Backpacking India with my Grandma

In Loving Memory of

Malcolm Ellis Davies (Dave)

Backpacking India with my Grandma

By Jake Pitts and Barbara Davies

Copyright © 2018

ISBN-13: 978-1720733713
ISBN-10: 1720733716

Chapter 1 – How it Happened

So, I think the best way to start the story of this backpacking journey through India with my Grandma is to explain how it happened, and just how it came about. As it's not everyday you decide to take your Grandma on your journey around India with you. India is a difficult country to travel anyway, with the heat, busy streets and change in culture. It can come as a massive shock, being very stressful at times.

Originally I had booked the whole trip myself. I booked my flights and got my visa, about 3 months prior to my Grandma even knowing I was coming to India. I had planned my trip, where I was going, what I wanted to see and had it all set out. I had it all booked and sorted when I was still in my second year of university. I had finished uni by now and had about 4 weeks at home before I set off. And of course, I go and visit everyone while I'm home. This one particular day I had planned to visit my Grandma. We were sitting and talking, as we do for hours, and came onto this one topic of bucket lists. We were discussing what we had always wanted to do, and things we had always wanted to see as my Grandad had passed away around 6 months prior. We were discussing how he had done and seen everything he wanted to see, and how he used to tell us that he lived his life to the fullest, and done everything he had always wanted to do.

Anyhow, me and Grandma were talking about bucket lists and of course, I was telling her all about my India trip, where I planned to go and what I planned to see. And of course mentioned the Taj Mahal. One of the seven wonders of the world, and she was saying about how it was on her bucket list, and she had always wanted to see it. She also mentioned about how she would probably never get the opportunity to go now. Mainly due to the fact not many of her friends would want to go, and she wouldn't want to go on her own.

Now I don't know whether it was in the moment or I was just feeling a little crazy, but I just randomly said, 'why don't you come'. Instantly she looked at me like I was crazy, and probably rightly so. She said 'I couldn't, I wouldn't be able to get a flight now'. I remember responding saying, 'yeah of course you could'.

I mean, I think I never expected her to actually

come, like it was just some wild proposition. Then before I know it she has her diary and money book out, and she's looking through it checking dates. She said she would think about it while we headed up the market.

After spending a few hours up the market within 5 minutes of returning back to my Grandmas house she said 'yeah I can come, I can afford it, if it's going to cost this much, why the hell not'.

In my head at first I was like 'Oh shit', this is actually happening, my Grandma is coming backpacking around India with me. It was more the shock than anything. When I woke up that morning, I would have never imagined my day would've turned out like that. So we decided to wait 2 days until she had sorted her money out, and then planned to meet to get everything booked.

By this time, I had, had plenty of time to think about it and the trip, and had let it sink in a little that I would be backpacking this country with my Grandma, and do you know what, I was pretty damn excited. I thought it would be such an incredible experience for us both, it would bring us closer, and we we're both bound to have an incredible time. I knew she was about as adventurous and fit as 68 Year old's get, so that wasn't a worry at all.

So the day came and it was time to get everything booked. It still hadn't fully sunk in, I don't think it did until we boarded the plane to be honest. I got out my laptop and all my emails, now the first challenge was trying to get her on the same flight as me. So I put in the dates and we hoped for the best, because she said if she couldn't get on the same flight, then she wouldn't want to go. Luckily the same flight popped up, with the same dates and same times, so we instantly booked it. It was a little more expensive than what mine cost, but she didn't seem to mind. The next challenge was applying for the Visa, we got out all her documents and took pictures of them all. We then uploaded them and got the visa applied for, which didn't take too long, we just had to hope it got approved.

Then we had to book travel insurance, now this was a little more expensive, trying to find the cheapest travel insurance for a 68 year old for 3 weeks in India. We just ended up using a comparison website, and selecting the best deal, I don't think it was too bad in the end, and only ended up costing about £40. So that was the flights, insurance, visas all booked and sorted. Just the hostel left to book, so we booked our first four nights in New Delhi so we knew where we were staying.

So everything was all booked, and pretty much ready to go, other than the visa being approved. Now throughout this process we agreed that we would stay in hostels. And Grandma was really easy going about the whole idea. She said she didn't mind what we did, or where we went. It was up to me to decide. And she said she didn't mind staying in and trying hostels. We booked ourselves into separate hostel rooms. I went for the cheapest biggest rooms, and she went for the smallest they weren't that much more expensive, but my budget was a little tighter than hers, and I suppose she wanted a bit more comfort, when her first experience of a hostel was at 68 years old, and of all countries, in India.

I then showed her the places I had planned to visit, and some of the things I had searched and thought would be amazing to see. She was really open, she said she didn't mind where we went, as long as she got to she the Taj Mahal, which was a given. After looking at all the amazing places we were going to visit, and some of the sights we were going to see, we both began to get pretty excited about the whole adventure.

About 4 days later the Visa was confirmed, and that was it. Everything was in place for us to go. I was pretty excited now as that was the last thing we were waiting on until we were ready to go.

Now everything was booked and confirmed, we could properly look forward to it.

Just 2 weeks and we would be on our way to India.

It all seemed to be a little more real now.

Me, My Grandma,

Backpacking,

India.

It was a normal Wednesday morning. Jake had come into Boston for the day. We were having a coffee before going into town to the market and talking about his Grandad, the places we had been and the fun we had when we took him and his sister away in our caravan. Jake then started to tell me about his plans for his forthcoming backpacking trip to India in about two and a half weeks.

"Your Grandad used to say that he'd like to go to India" said I. "I will be SO jealous when I see your pictures. I've always wanted to see the Taj Mahal, but it's too late now"

Jake just looked at me and said, "Why Grandma? Come with me!"

I was lost for words, which doesn't often happen! I tried to tell him that he didn't want an old biddy like me coming along cramping his style! After all, I was sixty-eight and he was twenty. He was having none of it. "Come on Grandma, it'll be fun. Let's go and make some new memories". I said that I would think about it and off we went to the market.

Well, I was thinking all morning, shall I or shan't I? I spoke to a couple of friends on the *market stalls and the general reaction was "grab it with both hands". One even offered to let me look after her stall while she went to India in my place. After a long morning of thinking, when we got home I finally said yes!*

The next morning I was back in Boston to make sure I had the money in my current account to cover all of the expenses involved in booking my trip. I then called in at the doctors to see if I needed any new vaccinations or boosters. I also needed a passport sized photo for my Indian visa. In the flurry of activity and excitement I forgot the all-important photo, so after lunch I had to take a quick trip back to town. I then drove out to see Jake, heart in mouth, butterflies in tummy and debit card in hand!

A couple of hours later and it was all booked and paid for. Jake had managed to get me the last seat on his flight, my visa was bought and the first hostel in Delhi sorted. I made it clear that I didn't want more than a six-bed room. It cost me a little more than a larger share, but what the heck! I went home in something of a daze!

Friday morning I woke up and thought, 'What the hell have I done!?'. Terror fought with excitement and those butterflies were really doing a fandango in my stomach. Would I cope with a backpack? Would I cope with sharing a room with total strangers? Not all of the rooms in hostels are single sex, so some of these strangers would probably be male! Most of all would I cope with the humidity and the heat and would I be able to avoid the dreaded 'delhi-belly'!? However, there was no time to worry about such minor details.

The next two weeks passed in a frenzy of activity. My daughter ordered a backpack for me online, as Jake considered my current one too small. He was right! I was told I only needed one booster, Typhoid, and this was fitted in for me as I didn't have much time. I bought sun cream, tummy pills and mosquito repellent. I didn't need the latter but better safe than sorry! I also invested in some loose, lightweight cotton clothes.

I lost count of the number of times that my backpack was packed and repacked. I added some extras and then took things out several times, but eventually I was satisfied. Just as well, as departure date was fast approaching. A few of my friends said, "Oh, I wouldn't fancy that", but the best reaction of the majority was, "Good for you! Go for it!"

June 5th soon arrived. My butterflies were now doing what felt like a jitterbug in clogs and I felt a mixture of nerves and excitement. However, excitement won as Jakes mum and dad arrived to collect me and off we went to the airport. The adventure had begun!

Chapter 2 – Flying Out

So the day was finally here, the day me and my Grandma were due to fly to India. Bags Packed and ready to leave. It was an early flight, at around 12am and from my family home it takes around 3 hours to get to the airport, so we had to be up pretty early, leaving at about 6am. My dad planned to take us and we picked up my Grandma on the way where she was waiting for us. The drive down was pretty long, I think I slept a little bit, but most of the journey was spent talking. About 3 hours later we arrived at the airport, so it was time for us to leave behind the comforts of home, and head of to the subcontinent of India. Me and Grandma hopped out of the car, grabbed our bags, said goodbye and off we headed into the airport. We walked in and decided to check in on the computers to save us queueing up. I got mine all done and sorted pretty quickly, and then got my Grandma sorted out, her passport scanned and put in the reference number, and then it printed out our boarding passes.

We then dropped our bags off, which made things so much easier, as now we weren't having to cart these heavy rucksacks around, and could wander around in more comfort. We then went through security which was pretty speedy and got a coffee while we waited for our flight. I was pretty excited now, for me once I have my boarding pass, it's all go and there isn't as much to worry about, you know you haven't forgotten anything important. We just sat and talked and planned what we were going to do, and said how crazy it was that we were going on this trip together. The craziest fact that 3 weeks ago, I thought I was going to be backpacking India solo, and my Grandma thought she would be at home in England.

We also said that if Grandad was looking down on us now, how he would laugh, and be incredibly happy for us.

Looking down, so proud of us both for seizing this adventure, and not saying no to the opportunity.

After sitting drinking coffee for a good hour, it was about time for us to leave and go find our flight. So we got up, grabbed our bags and went to look to find out what gate we were at. We walked to our gate and the plane was boarding, so after a quick visit to the toilet we boarded the plane, found our seats and were sat down. I was lucky enough to get a window seat which is my favourite, I love being able to look out the window, and look down at the world from above.

Before you know it were taxiing out on the runway, the planes picking up speed and the front end is of the ground.

I'm just sat there looking out the window, thinking wow, after 9 month's of studying and working, I finally have 4 months off to travel, and what an awesome way to start it by backpacking through India with my Grandma. I was just sat there looking down on little London from the small plane window. And I kept coming back to the same thought, 'my Grandma is sat next to me, and this plane is heading for India'. I still don't think it had really sunk fully in.

I have no idea what Grandma was thinking as we headed into the sky. Probably something very similar to me.

After about an hour or so of cruising through the air, they brought out our first meal. We both joked that the food we got on the plane would probably be our last meal that wasn't some sort of Indian food for over 2 weeks, so we should make the most of it, as neither of us knew what to expect. We both had some sort of chicken tomato dish with potatoes and veg. I love plane food anyway, so it was great. I then reclined my seat, stuck in my headphones and planned to watch a few films and chill out before landing in our first stop of Istanbul in Turkey, where we had an hour layover.

When I had finished watching a couple of movies I checked my phone to see what time it was in Turkey and how long we had left on our flight. Turned out we were running a bit late, and would be landing in Turkey at 3.45pm, Turkish time.

Well this was a little problem for us, as we were due to depart from Turkey at 4pm and begin our journey to Delhi. That would give us only 15 minutes to catch our connecting flight. It would probably take us that long to get of the plane, and then we had to find and get to the gate.

We were both sat there. My Grandma looked a little worried and I think was stressing a little bit. I just said it doesn't matter, if we miss it, we miss it. There is nothing we can possibly do about it, it's the airlines responsibility, and they will have to put us on the next flight if we do miss it. So there is no point worrying.

We landed in Istanbul at 3.45pm, and literally had 15 minutes to get of the plane, find our gate and board the next flight. I was thinking no chance, it's never going to happen, it could be a 30 minute walk to our gate alone. Let alone how long it was going to take us to get of the plane. I wasn't stressing at all, as I just thought there was no chance in hell of us making it, but still we thought we may as well try

So we grabbed our bags, and tried to get of the plane as quickly as possible, we briskly walked down the aisle of the plane, down the stairs to the outside. It turns out we have to wait for this bus to be loaded to take us to the departure lounge and gates. So we had to wait for the bus to be fully loaded before it could leave, I swear it seemed like everyone was taking their time on purpose, obviously they weren't, but it was frustrating.

After waiting here for about 7 ish minutes, the

bus left, and headed to departures.

I kept checking my watch wondering if we would make it, and wondering when the next flight with 2 free seats to Delhi might be.

The bus pulled up alongside two glass doors at about 3.55pm. We jumped of the bus, walked through the automatic doors, quickly showing our boarding passes to the Turkish security man.

I went straight to the departure board to find out what gate our flight was leaving from, silently praying that the gate wasn't further than a couple of minutes away, as we didn't have long left.

Turns out it was the gate next to the one were dropped of at.

Well shit, that was lucky.

There were about 4 people left in the queue for boarding. So after looking at Grandma and pointing and telling her the gate was right there, and seeing her face light up with relief, we jumped in the queue.

They checked our boarding passes and got us on the plane.

Within about 20 minutes, we were both in the air, drinking gin and tonic and finally on our way to New Delhi. Slightly sweaty, and still flustered at the whole rush and excitement of actually making the flight. Just 7 hours left and we'd be touching down in India.

Our flight was as uneventful as most flights are. Several hours of eating, drinking and watching different movies. The only excitement we had was in Istanbul. We had an hour and a half to transfer to our next flight. The only problem was that our flight from England was an hour late landing, so we had a mad dash across Istanbul airport. We made it by the skin of our teeth! Once on the plane we sat…. And sat! We were nearly another hour before we took off! Presumably it took that long to transfer the luggage from our original flight to all of the connecting flights. Once airborne the eating, drinking and watching different movies resumed. Jake may also have slept, but I never sleep on planes.

Chapter 3 – Day 1 New Delhi

After a 7 hour flight, which I think both of us slept for most of it, we touched down in New Delhi.

We arrived in Delhi at about 6am, so we were both feeling still a little drowsy and tired. We got boarded of the plane, and now we had to queue up to go through security and get our Visas checked.
We looked for the right line, the one that we were supposed to be in. The queues were actually really small, I guess because it was one of the first flights in of the day, there were only about 4-5 people in-front of us. We got in line and moved up to the security desk, I was a little nervous about this, I always do get a little nervous with visas. Just in case they reject it. We showed him the confirmation of our visas. He took photos of us and got our fingerprints, after about 20 minutes each we got through to the other side, got a stamp in our passport, and headed to baggage claim.

After about 15 minutes the baggage started to come out and slowly move around the carousel. Along came my bag and I grabbed it off.

About 15 minutes later and my Grandma still hadn't seen hers….

10 mins went by and she still hadn't seen it, she was starting to panic a little now, as she thought that they might have lost it, or got the bags mixed up with the fast transfer of planes in Turkey.

There were only about 7 bags left on the carousel at this point. So we waited another 5 mins and there was still no sign of it, we we're both starting to get a little worried.

About another 5 minutes when by when she says 'ohh there it is', and I grab this backpack of the carousel.

I look at it, turn my head towards her with this huge grin on my face and say 'this bloody bags been going around for the past 45 minutes', she just looks at me and says 'oh I must of forgotten what it looked like'. We both just laughed. I couldn't believe, we had both just been sat there for 45 minutes watching her bag go around, both of us oblivious to what it looked like. In all fairness she had just gotten the backpack a few days ago, but still, it was hilarious.

After collecting the bags we headed out of the airport. I already knew where we were going as I had looked it up in google maps, and knew what train we had to get on, and where we had to get off. We decided to use the local train system as we thought it would be a lot cheaper, turns out after a day of being in New Delhi, that it really wasn't that much cheaper and it was only 30p more each to get a tuk tuk. If only we had known this in advance it would have saved us a lot of hassle on the train.

After getting out of the airport and being immediately bombarded by taxi, tuk tuk, and whatever else, we headed for the train station. From the airport to the hostel we had to make one change at some station in the middle of the city. We found and got on the first train pretty easily and it was quite nice, it was quite and comfortable and we both managed to get a seat. We got of the first train and had to find our second train which took us to the hostel. By this time it was about 7.30am in the morning and I kid you not, this train station was heaving, I guess it was rush hour, with everyone going to work. We both had these pretty big backpacks on our backs and were trying to navigate our way around this absolutely packed train station at 7.30am in the morning, after getting very little sleep.

We finally found which train we had to be on, and what platform and in the right direction. When we got there there were loads of people down at the platform. The trains kept passing, but they were to busy for people to get on. Not even room for another body.

One guy told my Grandma that there was a special carriage at the back just for women, but she understandably didn't want to go, so we waited for each other. A train came up and there was a bit of room on it, so we squeezed ourselves in. We both took our backpacks off and kept them at our feet, this made it a bit easier to move around, and also gave us more space. The further out of central Delhi we got the quieter the train became, and the more room we had, thankfully. About 20 minutes later and we arrived at the stop we were due to get off at for our hostel. So we got of the train and headed for the streets to try and find our hostel.

Once of the train, we had to find our way to the

hostel, by now it was about 8am and the streets were pretty busy. I had a screen shot of where we had to walk and where the hostel was on my phone, so I could gauge a rough idea of the direction we were supposed to be walking.

I got it up and we started to follow it, it seemed pretty simple, it was a 10 minute walk down the street from the train station. After about 10 minutes of walking we still hadn't seen the hostel. We continued for another 10 minutes and the shops along the street came to an end, the path just continued as a dirt road with nothing either side of it.

I initially thought we had walked past it, so we walked back looking at the buildings to see if we could find it, but no luck. I re-checked the map on my phone and tried to get an idea of where we were stood. After a couple of minutes I figured we were on the wrong side of the road. We were supposed to be walking down the other side, out of the station and left. The road we had to cross was about 4 lanes wide, then there was a little gap in the middle where people could stand, then another 4 lanes of cars going in the opposite direction. The road was busy, and there was not many a chance to cross.

We pretty much just ran across with the locals, the cars and scooters still shooting past you. We got to the middle and just had four more lanes to cross. After being stood there for about 5 minutes we finally got a break, and made a dash for it.

We were both just looking forward to sitting in an air-conditioned room, by now we had been on the move from the airport for a couple of hours. After about 10 minutes of walking down the other side of the road, we saw a sign saying 'Joey's Hostel'.

We had finally made it to the hostel. Great.

There were these small stairs leading up, it didn't look much like a hostel, but we wandered up anyway. It was about two stories up when we finally got there, we walked into the hostel and there was just one guy sat at a desk, it looked much more like a hostel now. There were sofas, a television, a kitchen, tables and chairs and much to our delight the place was air-conditioned.

The lights were still off, they turned them on at about 8am I guess. We walked up to the desk got checked in, and then we just sat down and chilled for a minute, enjoyed the air conditioned room, and waited for breakfast to be laid out.

Breakfast was ready about 15 minutes later, and consisted of some sort of curry, which I didn't try for breakfast once. I just couldn't stomach the thought of curry for breakfast, even though we were in India, that just wasn't for me. My Grandma had it a couple of times, and she really enjoyed it, even after her good review, I still didn't try it. Coco pops, toast, jams and spreads. It was a pretty basic breakfast, but it did the job, after breakfast, which for me consisted of about 4 bowls of coco pops, and my Grandma toast and jam. We both went and got our stuff unpacked, showered and got ready for the day ahead, our first day in India. We thought we may as well get out and get exploring since we were already up.

We got a city map and decided we would head into the old city and walk around and walk to the red fort. So we headed outside and went train station, then got on the next train to Delhi central. Once at Delhi central train station we thought it would be nice to walk through the old city, and walk to the red fort, the walk was about 2 hours in total. We started our walk through the winding streets of Delhi, past all these little stalls selling spices and different snacks.

While walking through the streets the smell constantly changed, one minute you would get the lovely smell of nice Indian foods and spices that would make your taste buds tingle, then you would turn a corner and it would smell like a sewage treatment plant. You would physically have to hold your nose to stop yourself from being sick.

We kept walking through the old city, which was really beautiful, all the old red buildings, and stone work with random paintings on them, there were also lots of different temples on the way. It was such a contrast, walking from the reasonably modern part of Delhi to the old town. The old town was made up of markets and stalls, and shops built into walls, the stalls were selling everything imaginable from samosas to shoe laces.

It was about 12 noon so it was getting really hot, the fact it was also summer in India probably didn't help, let alone the fact that it was our first day in India.

It was around 40c, and we were both sweating from head to toe. I mean, I was finding the heat quite exhausting so I could only feel for my Grandma. We had been walking for about an hour and a half through New Delhi, and around the old city.

We were heading for the red fort. This is a really famous architectural fort, and one of the must see things in New Delhi. We weren't really sure how far away we were, as all I had was this map from my phone in my hand, and they're never really specific, so it's hard to guess a time and judge how far away you are.

About 30 minutes later we arrived and could see the red fort, we were both a bit flustered from the heat, and had come across a section of street that was all markets, so kept getting hassled and pestered to buy things.

I could see my Grandma was getting a little bit hot and bothered, so I suggested we find somewhere to sit and grab a drink. I mean it probably wasn't the best idea to walk for 2 hours across New Delhi, in midday heat, on our first day in India, with little sleep but it definitely helped us acclimatise.

We walked and walked and couldn't find anywhere to sit and have a drink, it was all stalls and shops. Eventually we found one, so we walked in sat down and ordered two cold drinks, then the guy, presumably who owned the restaurant, starts asking us about food. We both said no we don't want food multiple times, and just wanted a drink, but he wasn't having any of it. He kept pestering us to buy food. After about 5 minutes of this, I just said, look, we don't want anything, my Grandma just needs to sit down for a little while in the shade. He got the idea and just left us alone. The restaurant was empty anyway, so it wasn't like we were losing him money.

After just sitting there for about 10 minutes enjoying the shade, and enjoying not being in that belting midday Indian heat, we got up and headed for the fort. We thought we would grab a drink from a store outside. We both decided to get a large cold mango juice, and it tasted amazing.

After grabbing a drink we headed up to the fort.

There were about 50 steps to climb to get up to the top, when at the top we had to pay an entrance fee to get a ticket, then we could go in. In India, it was always about 10x the price for foreigners than it is for locals to enter things like temples, museums, national parks. So for locals it was free, whereas for us it was 300 rupees.

After paying and collecting our tickets, we got to the entrance. We had to take of our shoes, out of respect, as you do in many temples in India. And my Grandma also had to cover her shoulders. When we got inside there were loads of places to sit around the edge, there were a few people sleeping, as it was in the shade. So we decided to head over to the shade and sit and chill before we looked around the fort. We had just walked for over 2 hours in this heat, and a little rest and lay down sounded perfect to the both of us.

After taking my rucksack of, which I used as a makeshift pillow, I laid back in the shade, put my cap over my eyes and closed them. It felt so nice to just lay down and close my eyes, considering we had been up so early, fresh of a red eye flight and had just done this 2 hour walk through India on our first day.

I remember just laying there, having all these different feelings and thoughts going through my head, of being in India, and having 4 months of from uni, it felt incredible.

After what felt like just five minutes, I lifted the cap of my head and sat up. Checked my phone and it had been 35 minutes. My Grandma was still sat there looking around, and looked so excited about the prospect of being in India. And I'm sure she'll mention the fact that I fell asleep for 30 minutes while laying there, it was a comfy spot, what can I say.

We decided to get up and have a look around the fort, which was absolutely magnificent, brick red walls and dome shaped towers, then there were big sections of water throughout the middle. The fort wasn't huge, and there wasn't a lot to look around, it was mainly just a big square in the middle, and then a prayer room at one end. By the time we had finished looking around, it was about 3pm.

We got our shoes back, and proceeded to walk down the stairs at the entrance of the temple.

After getting almost to the bottom of the 50 stairs. Me, being the clumsy person I am somehow stumbled and tripped, and managed to split the end of my big toe open, fair to say I didn't wear flip flops again. I had to grab onto my Grandma to stop myself from falling all the way over and doing a little roll.

I mean you would've expected it to be the other way around, not the 20 year old falling and injuring himself... my Grandma loves to tell this story, as you can imagine.

Before I knew it I had about 10 Indians around me helping me over to this little shelter at the entrance to the fort. To be honest, it was a little embarrassing, I mean I could still walk, with a little limp. It did hurt though, my big toe was throbbing, but I could still get myself about. I was more worried about all the dirt getting into the wound.

Once I was sat down on this little stool, the guy was saying he was going to get some bandage and some water. One guy grabbed my leg and some old rag of the floor and went to wipe my toe and the blood with it. I kid you not, I have never moved my leg so fast. I was like noo it's dirty. I mean who knows what that had been used for. I know he meant well, but he literally picked up some random cloth of the floor, it looked like it had been used to clean a car engine.

I got some water out of my bag and washed it over my big toe, rinsing out all the dirt from the slice in the end of it, then wrapped it up with a bandage this kind Indian guy had found me and tied it up. My toe was throbbing, so once I had managed to stop the bleeding, we decided it was probably time for us to head back to the hostel. So one of the kind guys got us a tuk tuk, we agreed a fare price and off we shot back to the hostel.

Once we got to the hostel, and I had managed to limp my way up the stairs, we were hot sweaty and well I had a bloodied toe, so we decided we would shower and meet in the common area in about an hour, then chill before going and grabbing our first Indian meal.

I headed up to my room, and gave my toe a good wash in the shower, it hurt like hell scrubbing it with soap. But I wanted to properly clean it out. I was worried about all the dirt that may have gotten inside it, from the roads, paths and tuk tuk. After cleaning it out, and finishing my shower. I re bandaged it properly up and it felt much better, as-well as me being a lot cleaner and not having clothes on that were covered in sweat. After sorting all that out, I headed back downstairs to meet my Grandma, to find she was sat there waiting, reading her book.

We got sat down and just chilled and spoke for an hour or so about our first day and had a little plan about what we were going to do tomorrow. It was about 7pm by this time, and we decided it was time for us to go and try our first local Indian dinner.

We headed out and walked down the street, we were in an area called Laxmi Nagar, which was where the hostel was located.

We walked for about 15 minutes looking into each restaurant and seeing if it took our fancy, there was a lot of choice, every other building was a local eatery. We finally decided on this little place which was really busy and seemed to have some good choices. We had both decided to be vegetarian throughout our trip, as we had heard some stories about the meat and because of dodgy refrigeration it can cause you to get really bad food poisoning. So we decided to stay clear of it.

Once in the restaurant we sat down and both got a menu. We both looked at it and had no idea what any of the dishes meant or what they consisted of. So we asked the guy which ones were the vegetarian dishes and he told us they were all vegetarian, which was perfect. It was really just a guessing game, we had to just pick at random and hope we liked it, luckily we did. We decided to buy two dishes and just share them both. We picked a stuffed paratha, which was like a stuffed flat-bread, filled with potatoes, onions and some masala style thick sauce. Then we also got a plain dosa which came with a couple of sauces to dip it in, this was a kind of thin flat pancake. It was nice, but tasted kind of plain. You just dipped in in this chilli sauce and it came with some green vegtable soup, which was pretty tasty. The paratha was definitely my favourite dish, the dosa not so much, just due to tasteless flavour.

All of the dishes came with no cutlery so we weren't really sure how to eat it. We kind of just kept looking around, and watching the locals eat, and tried to copy what they were doing, I still managed to get curry, soup and sauces all over my fingers and hands. Grandma seemed to get the hang of it pretty quickly. After finishing our meal and paying around £2 for it all including two drinks, we decided to leave and head back to the hostel.

By the time we got back to the hostel it was about 20.30 and even though it was super early we both decided it would be a good idea to go and get some sleep, especially since it had been a long day, we had been up super early, and we also wanted a good nights rest for the next day. So after walking back the same way we came, we decided to go up to sleep and arranged to meet for breakfast at 9am. As soon as my head hit the pillow I fell asleep, and didn't open an eye lid until 8am.

Eventually we landed in Delhi in the early hours of the morning. We stepped off the plane into what felt like a sauna; heat and humidity. Still being dressed for an English 'summer' we were glad to get inside the air-conditioned terminal. After having our passports and visas examined we finally made it to baggage retrieval. Jakes bag came quite quickly, but mine seemed to take forever! I got quite worried, thinking that it had been put on the wrong aircraft in Istanbul, or even that it was still sitting in London or Turkey! Suddenly I realised (with a little help from Jake) that the black backpack that had been round two or three times was mine! (in my defence I had only had it about a week and I thought it had some red on it!) The relief to have my backpack was worth the teasing I had to put up with from Jake. I got revenge later!

We then made our way to the railway station, having decided to take the train to our first hostel, Joey's. What an experience! Japan's commuter trains pale into insignificance by comparison! The railway started off underground, with fenced rails and gateways for dissembling and boarding and everyone keeping right to avoid the rushing of people. I managed to board the first train that came but Jake thought that there wasn't enough room for him so he refused. I wasn't going without him so I got off... and at least three or four more people got on in my place. This meant that we were first in the queue, however, so we boarded the next one quite comfortably. As we were approaching our station, by this time overground and literally on stilts, Jake spotted Joey's, so at least we knew which way to head when we got off. It was still dark and we had to wake the young lad manning the desk overnight. Our beds were still occupied, naturally at that time in the morning, but we were assured that they would be freshly made up for us before nightfall. We were able to leave our bags and were also assured of breakfast, which was included in the price in most hotels. We had to wait a while as no-one was up yet, but a cuppa was most welcome after travelling all night.

After breakfast (cereal, bananas and toast, although I did have curry one morning!) did we take the opportunity to catch up on some much needed sleep? Oh no! We decided to go into Delhi and explore! We took a scooter-like rickshaw, called a tuk-tuk, into the city and, being green, paid 100 rupee's each. Never again! One of the sights on the agenda was a place called the Red Fort, so we decided to try and find it. On enquiry we were told it was half an hour to and hour away, so we set off to walk. Hours must be longer in India as two hours later we were still walking, but we did see some areas of Delhi where it seemed that tourists never find, which was fascinating. However, after a sleepless night and in 40 degree heat I was flagging slightly, but I was determined not to hold Jake back so I kept going. We were hoping to be able to buy some water but there were no shops in sight, only stray dogs and sacred cows. Eventually we reached the Fort, and shops and cafes. We went into a cafe to cool down and asked for a drink, but the owner was determined that we should have something to eat. We were equally determined that we just wanted a drink, so the next thing we know he turned the fans off! As we were obviously not going to get our drink we left, went next door and bought bottled water and some mango juice.

We were just walking towards the fort and a guy stopped and asked us and asked if I was Jakes mother. On learning I was his Grandmother he did something I found amazing, he said 'don't be alarmed or offended this is how we show our respect', he then proceeded to kiss his fingers and touch my feet. Far from being offended I felt touched and honoured. This is typical of the reaction I experienced in this amazing country.

I had been told that in India you only had to cover your head in holy places, but this must only apply to Sikh Temples. The Red Fort turned out to be a Mosque. I not only had to wear a long stifling robe but also borrow Jakes spare socks as I had to take my sandals off and the marble floor was red hot. Luckily Jake got away with just removing his flip flops. We sat a while in the shade enjoying our juice then, refreshed, set out to explore this amazing place. The fort glowed like a ruby in the afternoon sun and the white marble floor dazzled our eyes. Jake attracted the attention of a gang of small boys, who wanted their pictures taken with him.

After an hour or so we decided it was time to go, so we reclaimed our footwear and started down the steps leading to the gate. I was ahead of Jake, but suddenly I heard an exclamation from behind.

I turned around to see Jake picking himself up and blood pouring from his big toe! He hobbled to the bottom of the steps, where he was soon surrounded by several very helpful Indians. One found him a chair, but he politely turned down the filthy rag another was offering him to stop the blood as I had tissues in my bag.

(Never leave without them in India, just in case!) We dealt with the bleeding as best we could and someone appeared with some plasters. Someone else insisted on finding us a tuk-tuk which was how we discovered we only needed to pay 50 rupee's each for a journey twice as long as the original one.

I just couldn't resist my turn to tease! After all, the sixty-eight year old was still on her feet but the twenty year old had come a cropper! I was, however, a bit concerned about the dirt and the heat, but Jake assured me he healed quickly and would be fine. He was right, two days later there was no sign of any injury, but Jake never wore flip flops again!

Back at the hostel we collected our bags and were taken to our rooms. I was in a six-bed dorm on the main floor, but Jake was up more narrow stairs in a ten-bed dorm. After we had settled in we went out to explore the area. What an eye-opener. During the day it had been relatively quiet but the evening was another story. On a pathway about the width of a narrow single track country lane and lined with shops and cafes one side and various stalls the other, tuk-tuks, cycle rickshaws, scooters, motorbikes and pedestrians all jostled for space in the two-way traffic! There was even the occasional car squeezing by. It was noisy, bustling and exciting and like nothing I have ever experienced in all of my travels. That evening I was introduced to the music of Delhi, and every other Indian city if the truth be told. Car horns! Incessant and loud! Even using pedestrian crossings we were hooted by motorists who didn't want to stop.

After some time spent exploring we went into a local cafe and had a wonderful meal. We ate a pancake-like dish with a soup-like dip and a creamy but spicy one. I really can't remember what they were called but Jake will. It was ridiculously cheap, under £3 for us both, with a drink, but it was one of the dearer meals that we had in Delhi. Then it was back to Joey's and bed for some much needed sleep in readiness for the next exciting day of our adventure.

Chapter 4 – Day 2 New Delhi

Today we woke up and did the usual again, got showered, got all our stuff ready for our second day in New Delhi, and met for breakfast at around 9am, I had decided to wear trainers rather than flip-flops after yesterdays stumble, and unfortunate toe splitting open. We both felt so much better after getting a good nights sleep, around 11-12 hours to be exact. It was definitely needed after the long day we had before, getting in early on the flight and exploring India for our first day, the rest was definitely needed. I think the heat also makes you more tired in general, when it is 40c outside, you just feel a lot more tired.

After getting breakfast and planning where we were going for the day we grabbed our bags and headed out into the sun, we got half way down the road and I realised I had forgotten my sunglasses, which was annoying as it was too far to turn back and grab them, but the sun was super bright and it was hard to see at times, so I was just squinting, that was until my eyes adjusted to the light. We grabbed a tuk tuk, and after a few mins of bartering we got a good price. The tuk tuks turned out to be pretty cheap, especially when the price was split between two it was only a little more expensive than getting on the train, so it made sense to just use a tuk tuk. They were a hell of a lot more convenient too.

Today we decided to head to the Lodi Gardens for the morning. Which is a big city park, with monuments, tombs and temples inside. So after getting the tuk tuk there, we hopped out, paid the guy and went into the gardens. From the entrance it looked like it cost to get in, as there were some security guards stood there, it looked as if you had to pay them. We just walked past and they didn't say anything to us, so I presume that they were just there for security. We walked inside and there was a map of the gardens, so we kind of planned a little route and started to walk around. It was really beautiful inside. It was surprisingly bright green and there were loads of different trees and animals running about, it was slightly cooler than being in the city. I guess because of the shade from the trees. It also felt incredibly peaceful. I think the quietness made it seem a lot more peaceful, as Delhi is a really loud city, with the constant beeping of horns, and shouting of people.

We just strolled around the gardens, going in each of the individual tombs and exploring and walking around, it was really nice, just wandering around and talking. After about 2 hours, god knows where the time went, we had about finished in the gardens so decided to leave and go and get a drink somewhere cool, as we both already had a good sweat on, even through being in the shade the majority of the walk.

We left the gardens and just around the corner was this nice little bar/café, it looked really nice, so we decided to go inside and get a drink. We walked through the entrance to the café and went and sat down in the corner. The cold air-con hit us both right in the face, it was perfect. It was so nice to sit down and feel the cool air, feel almost fresh again. We both ordered some sort of soda, and again sat there for about an hour, just enjoying the cool feel of the room and enjoying our drink. They also brought us a wet towel which we used to wash over our face. The place was pretty expensive for India, but we thought it was worth it. After about an hour we decided to get the bill.

The bill came over and to our shock, it was a lot

more expensive that what the prices had shown, like expensive even for London standards. After looking at the bill, it seems they had added on service charge, tax, and a bunch of other things I have no idea what they meant, we asked and they said that was what we had to pay. So after unwillingly paying, making use of the normal toilets and getting a last feel of the cool fresh air, we headed back outdoors. The heat hitting our faces harder than the cool air when walking in.

We had decided that in the afternoon we would go and see the India Gate. So after leaving the restaurant, we headed to the road and grabbed a tuk tuk, after again haggling a price, which became almost routine, of we sped to the India Gate. The tuk tuk's used to vary on quality, the ones with leather seats were just awful, as your body would just stick to them, after sitting on it for 30 minutes it was like peeling tape of a wall, it was horrid. If we managed to get cushioned fabric seats we were in luck. The tuk tuk's were also a pretty scary experience at times, speeding through the lanes, ducking and dodging traffic. There were no, or very few traffic lights or road controls in New Delhi, it was more of a free for all. So when you're in this little motorbike style thing, it was definitely a little scary at times, even more so when you drive past and see one on it's side, because it took a corner to fast.

About 20 minutes later we arrived at the India Gate. Which is basically a large war memorial. After walking around here and taking a few pictures. We decided we would have a walk up the long gardens up to where the parliament of India was. After walking for about 20 minutes I was desperate for the toilet, now obviously I had to find somewhere, we walked for about 10 more minutes and came across a public toilet. I was pretty desperate so I had to brave it, I was literally 30 seconds, these toilets were dreadful, as in I physically couldn't even breathe they smelt that bad and I'm not exaggerating. It was a quick in and out situation. I could see a few of the locals smirking at me as I came out, red faced and gasping for air.

We continued walking down the gardens, and both felt like we were pretty hungry, as we hadn't had lunch yet. I really fancied one of those vegetable samosas. Which smelt and looked amazing, they basically fry them up in huge pots at the side of the street, and cook around 50 at a time. Along with lots of other different types of foods. The thing with buying these of the street though was that you wanted to buy them fresh, like literally as soon as they had been fried. Because otherwise they would've been left there on the side standing out, and there were a lot of flies and bugs about. It would almost have definitely given you a dodgy stomach. I think the heat makes you a lot less hungry, I'm not sure why but we just seemed to eat a lot less throughout the duration of the trip. Even though we were up and about and seemed to be doing more than we would if we were at home, most days we seemed to just skip lunch altogether.

We continued to walk towards the Indian parliament buildings. There was a big road down the middle leading up to the buildings from the India gate, and then like a garden area with water, or pools in straight lines, which weren't very deep, probably around 4ft. We were walking along the grass near to the water and there were a load of kids playing, it was super hot so I guess they were cooling down. They were completely naked, just jumping around and seemed to be having fun, they kept waving and smiling and flashing at us, which made us both laugh.

Still super hungry as we hadn't eaten since breakfast and it was now 3.30, we decided to head back towards the hostel area, as we knew there were places where we could find some food. We waved down a tuk tuk, of which there never seemed to be any when you wanted one. Literally all you would see while walking around on the roads, would be tuk tuks, until you needed one, and they seemed to reduce in numbers.

After about 10 minutes we managed to get one, hoped in and headed back to the hostel area. Unfortunately the tuk tuk had leather seats, and after spending the day walking around Delhi in the heat, we stuck to it pretty well.

Once arriving back in Laxmi Nagar, which is the area where our hostel was, our first mission was to find something to eat. We didn't want anything to big as it would only be a few hours before we went for dinner, but wanted something substantial enough to fill us for an hour or so. We had a little walk around and decided on this little samosa stand. We got them when they were fresh out of the pan, and he gave us a pot full of chilli sauce, and I kid you not, but it was the best samosa I have ever tasted. We went for a vegetable one, as I mentioned before, because the meat standards weren't supposed to be very good, and neither of us wanted to risk getting ill. It was filled with potatoes and all sorts of vegetables and spices, it was incredible, and it definitely didn't let us down.

We couldn't find anywhere to sit down to eat our samosa. The street was rammed, there wasn't even anywhere to stand, people were walking and riding scooters down the road, there wasn't really even any room to walk down the path, even more so as the street was packed with stalls selling you stuff. We found a spot just near the road under the railway bridge, that was reasonably, quiet isn't the right word to use, but I guess just less busy, and ate our samosas.

We headed back to the hostel to chill for a few hours, as we had been out in the sun all day, we both wanted to grab a shower and just chill out. So we did the same as usual, went back, grabbed a shower and just chilled out for a few hours. We played some cards, I used the Wifi and had a little plan and look at what we should do for the next day, and also got back to everyone that had messaged me.

After a few hours of relaxing we decided to go and grab some dinner. We left the hostel and headed for the streets again. It felt like this street literally never slept when it was dark, it was always busy at night, there were people all around, goods being sold, and restaurants were open, it was quite outstanding, how it was alive so constantly.

After walking around and down the street for a little while we couldn't seem to find anything that took our fancy, so we switched sides of the road and headed down the other side. This road was massive, it wasn't really in lanes but if it was, I would say it was probably about 8 in total, so four going each way, and a little gap for people to wait in the middle. As I have mentioned before, there were no traffic lights or crossings, it was literally a run for your life kind of thing. Making a break for it when there was no traffic, which wasn't often. You often just saw people walking across not even caring for the traffic that was trying to swerve around them.

After about 10 minutes, we were finally across

the road, and walked down the street looking for somewhere to eat. We finally found a little place, which looked pretty busy and so we headed in, and decided to grab some food. The food was similar to what we had the evening before. So we thought we would just try the different style of paratha and we also tried an uttapam. The uttapam was really nice, it's basically like a thick pancake and then it has all different styles of toppings. The guy that was cooking them, was cooking them on a big stove outside, and the restaurant was situated inside. Everyone was usually always really polite and nice, and the waiters would always move the fan so it was pointing on us. He could probably see the sweat dripping down our faces as we were ordering the food. The place was rammed, there were literally people waiting outside for a seat, so after we ate and finished our plates, we left.

We thought we may as well take a little walk down the street, as it was still quite early, about 8pm. And we may as well make the most of being on the other side of the road, seen as how long it took us to cross. We had a little walk all the way down the street, we were constantly beeped by scooters trying to squeeze past us on the pavement, as well as bicycles and even the occasional animal. You really did have to keep looking over your shoulder, every time you stepped out, you have to check to see if there is anything flying up the inside, otherwise you risk being knocked over.

When walking we noticed there were loads of little dessert shops, they would sell all kinds of like little deserts. These places seemed to be really busy and full of customers, so we thought we would go in one and try a few. As we walked in people were buying and pointing to the big cabinets in-front of the shop workers, who were stood behind them. They were basically big glass containers, full of all little finger sized cakes, sweets, jelly's and all other kinds of desserts you could imagine. All in different colours and with different toppings some had different fruits or nuts on the top of them, while some were just plain. We didn't even know where to start, we had no idea what was in them, or what flavour they where, and definitely had no hope of knowing what they tasted like.

After having a little look around, me and my Grandma, decided we would just pick two each and then split them in half, so four in total. So we both decided on two that looked nice and I went up and asked the guy if I could just have one of each. He looked at me kind of funny, as if it wasn't a normal thing to buy just two, but he smiled anyway, spoke to his colleague I guess they were discussing a price, and then he came back to me and said a number. It seemed pretty reasonable, in pounds it was about 50p. I gave the guy what I owed him and we headed outside to try them. The first one was really nice and we both liked it, it was a chocolate kind of flavour soft desert. The second was like a green looking desert, this was one that my Grandma picked, it was really strange tasting, kind of like kiwi flavour, but who knows. The second one again was one which my Grandma picked and was a chocolate looking one, it turned out to be like a coffee flavour, it was actually really nice, probably my favourite of the four we picked, it was more of a fudge consistency, and tasted amazing. The last one was some sort of fruity tart one which I picked, again this one was pretty nice too.

After finishing our desserts, it was getting on for 9pm and we both decided we should start walking back, and try to cross that road again.

We actually got across the road pretty quickly this time, we just ran across when the locals did, and kind of hoped for the best. We walked down the street past the same stalls that seemed to be there every night. Still it seemed like the street would never slow, it felt like it was constantly busy, especially late at night. It was full of people, socialising and eating. I guess that it's too hot in the day for people to be out doing things, so the locals tend to do it at night, when it's much cooler.

We got back to the hostel about 9pm. We decided we would chill for a little while, we played some more cards for about an hour, and then I decided I would go up to bed. I was shattered again, I guess being in the heat all day really does take it out of you. The temperature was hitting the low 40's. After talking to some of the Indians that lived in New Delhi, we found even the locals find it unbearably hot in the summer, many of them head to the north where it is cooler for holidays.

After a good nights sleep we woke up fairly early the next morning, refreshed and ready for more exploring. We were like the 'mad dogs and Englishmen' of the song, we were out everyday in the midday sun. We would leave the hostel about 10:30am-ish and return around four and five.

Our first stop this day was the India Gate, India's war memorial. I thought it was very reminiscent of Marble Arch, but made of what looked like sandstone. I found it very moving, as all memorials honouring the fallen are, but it was also vibrant and bustling with visitors from all over India. Afterwards we walked through a shady park opposite. It was also bustling with life, with families strolling and picnicking. A water-way ran through it, and many Indian boys were taking the chance to cool off in it, totally and unselfconsciously naked.

We then went onto a place called Loki Park. This was a scorching open space where we found ancient Mosques and Temples. How so many came to be built in the one area I have no idea! One avenue was guarded by two rows of palm trees, like soldiers on sentry duty. The ancient buildings were all awe inspiring, but after the first four or so we were asking each other, "have we seen this one?" They were all different, but so many seemed to numb the sense. I needed to check out my photos afterwards to sort them all out! We also found a pretty walled bonsai garden. I was fascinated by a miniature rhododendron, this was where we made our first acquaintance with the wild chipmunk population of India. Large feeding stations meant that they were used to people and so tame they would come within inches of our feet.

On our way in we had spotted a lovely cool looking cafe with a pretty paved garden, so we decided to have a cold drink and enjoy the air conditioning for a while on the way out. It was an expensive cool-down. Unlike the street-side cafes near to the hostel, a drink costing 150 rupee's on the menu, came in at about 300 rupee's after taxes and other additions.

Our tuk-tuk driver home was a very nice Sikh gentleman. He spoke of the many sights of Delhi too far away to walk to, so we struck a deal to hire him for the whole day the following day. After another excellent, ridiculously cheap meal and a few games of cards and poker-dice it was off to bed.

Chapter 5 – Day 3 New Delhi

Today was our third day in Delhi, we decided we would hire a tuk tuk driver for the day and get him to show us around some of the local places. So we got up, did the same routine, showered, dressed, covered ourselves in sun cream, and had a breakfast that consisted of coco pops and black tea. Although my Grandma was brave enough to try the curry for breakfast, this didn't take my fancy so much, especially seeing as I had a little case of Delhi belly. Delhi belly is when you get stomach ache, it's because your stomach is not used to the food and water, and it can be seriously painful. People often get quite ill from it when first visiting India, especially if you're not careful with what you eat and drink tap water.

Grandma said the curry was really nice, and that she would probably have it again, I still couldn't think about eating curry. Firstly I just couldn't fancy it for breakfast. Secondly, I just don't think my stomach could handle it first thing in the morning, so I stuck with coco pops.

After breakfast we headed to the streets, and met the tuk tuk driver. We arranged with the tuk

tuk driver the day before that we would meet at ten. He had dropped us off the afternoon before, we had agreed a price, and that he would take us around to all these different places for the day. It seemed pretty reasonable so we agreed to it, and decided to meet him the next day.

We walked down the street to where we was supposed to be meeting this guy, and there he was waiting next to his tuk tuk, he seemed happy to see us, obviously I guess as it meant he was getting paid today.

We jumped in the tuk tuk and headed to the first stop on our little tuk tuk trip, which was the lotus temple. After swerving in and out of loads of little roads for about 30 minutes we finally arrived, he said he would be waiting outside for us, so we got out and headed to the temple. The lotus temple is basically a big white flower like temple, it was pretty cool to look at. It reminded me of a smaller, less extravagant Sydney opera house. It's the place of Baha'i worship, and is surrounded by lots of gardens, water style lane ways and rectangular ponds leading up to it, it was quite beautiful. It was also free to visit, which was a bonus. We headed into the temple museum to start with, which my Grandma seemed to be more interested in than me, we had a little walk around and read some of the information about the religion. I was more enjoying the air-conditioned building that the museum was situated in, which was a blessing, as it was really hot this day. Not that it was cool on any day though, it just felt more humid some days.

After pondering about the museum and me subtly trying to hurry my Grandma up, we headed outside again, and began walking up towards the temple. It really was quite a magnificent building, unlike anything else in New Delhi city. Upon reaching it there was a bit of queue to get inside, but we thought we may as-well have a look. The unfortunate thing was that they asked you to take your shoes of as it was a holy place of worship, but the ground was scorching hot. They had laid down some wet mats as to make the ground not so hot, but it really didn't seem to help our feet, so we kept trying to get into the shade while staying in the queue. To add to the tease of the air conditioned building, there were pools full of water all around the temple, it was so tempting to just jump in one to cool down, it looked so refreshing, particularly when I had sweat dripping down my forehead. Somehow, I don't think they would've taken it very well though.

After about 20 minutes of waiting we headed inside the temple, where they did a prayer reading for about 10 minutes and we got to look inside. The inside was really amazing, I guess it was built in a way that amplified the voice, so during song and prayer reading everyone could hear clearly. Its design was really impressively. The prayer finished and it was time for us to leave, so we headed out of the temple and back down the same way we came up. We decided we would use the nice toilets in the museum again, as who knows when we would get toilets like that again, and then headed back through the gardens, and along the ponds to the tuk tuk driver. When travelling a place like India you learn to appreciate smaller things like clean toilets, you become even more grateful for this when arriving back home.

We found our tuk tuk driver, and we headed to the next stop on our trip, which was the national Gandhi museum. This I found really interesting, it was again free to enter and there was information on what Gandhi did and how he changed India. We then drove for about 15 more minutes and headed to the Raj Ghat, which is Gandhi's burial place. There was a memorial in the centre and it was surrounded by green gardens, with the occasional tree dotted within.

Upon entering, you had to take your shoes of. I guess as a sign of respect, as you have to for a lot of the temples and special sites throughout India. We handed in our shoes at the entrance to the site, walked around the gardens and took it all in. It was a quite, peaceful place, I guess that's the feel they were going for. There was no need to spend a long time there as there wasn't a great deal to see, so after 15 minutes we collected our shoes and headed back through the entrance.

Upon leaving we collected our shoes and the guy seemed to want a tip as for looking after them, so we gave him some small change and he didn't seem happy with it. He looked at us and kind of put his hand out asking for more, and got a bit annoyed with us. Even though it said it was free to put your shoes in there, I guess that's how he got his pay and made a living but he did get really upset with us. We decided to just leave, so we put our shoes on and walked swiftly back to the tuk tuk.

We then drove for quite a while as we were heading to Qutb Minar which was a little out of the centre of the city. We drove for about 35 minutes until we arrived. Qutb Minar is a 73 meter, 5 storey minaret that forms part of the Qutb complex, a UNESCO World Heritage Site.

Once we arrived we headed towards the entrance, turns out it was actually really expensive to go inside, the reason being as it was a world heritage site. We thought we would pass, as we had already spent a lot on the tuk tuk for the day, and you could see the minaret from outside the gates that surrounded the complex. It was 5 storeys high, so it was not like you had to go inside to see it. We just decided to walk around the outside, and had a little walk around the local area for about 30 minutes, there were a lot of ruins around the outside that we could see, so we were really glad we didn't pay to go inside, as we felt it wouldn't have been worth it. We grabbed a drink of a little stall, we always went for mango juice. It was so much more refreshing than soda or water, and was really cheap. I think in pounds it would've been about 30 pence. It tasted so good, especially when it was chilled.

We would often walk for 20 minutes just to find a shop with a refrigerator so we could get a cold one.

We headed back to the tuk tuk after about 30 minutes of walking around, and he was there again waiting for us. Out of pure randomness, I asked him if I could drive his tuk tuk. I thought it would be super cool to be able to drive one, you see them all around Asia, so it was kind of a novelty. He agreed and seemed quite excited about the fact I was driving his tuk tuk. I didn't go far, and it was actually really hard to steer, I just went up the road a little turned it around and came back, it wasn't easy to drive at all. I have no idea how they handle them so swiftly on the busy roads of Delhi, the steering was super stiff. I dread to think how they swerve in and out of traffic in these things. The driver asked my Grandma if she wanted a go, her response was a rather quick 'err no thank you, not for me', and that probably was the only thing she said no to our whole trip.

We jumped back into the tuk tuk and began heading back into the city of New Delhi.

When heading back into the city as it was about

4.30, and our day with the tuk tuk driver was coming to an end, when he kindly asked us if we wanted to go and look around a Sikh temple. Me and Grandma just looked at each other and kind of gave each other that look... yeah, why not. So off we headed to this Sikh temple.

We headed down to the foreign section where we had to register. It was also where we could leave our shoes and we had to wrap/cover our heads. We were like this guys two little followers, we literally had no idea what we were doing, or where we were going.

This temple was huge, and really outstanding, there was a big section in the middle which was a prayer room I guessed, where loads of people gathered to pray. Inside was beautiful, all gold, and decorated beautifully. Each little feature was so delicately crafted, we just stood at the back and gazed our eyes around while he went to pray. Everyone was really friendly, one young Indian girl even came and spoke to us and told us what was going on. She asked us where we were from and we had a little conversation at the back of the temple. Everyone seemed more than happy that we were there.

The outside area to the temple was huge. It had a sort of huge pond in the middle and then a walkway all around the outside. It was such a crazy thing to have in a temple, you just walked out the back and there it was this amazing peaceful place, right in the centre of New Delhi.

The Sikh tuk tuk driver, I would refer to him by his name, but I can't remember what it was for the life of me. He asked if we wanted to go and get some food, as they give you it for free in the temple, we said yes and thank you, and followed him, not knowing what to expect. We were both a bit sceptical at start, as we were only eating vegetarian food, so I asked, as I really didn't want to eat meat and end up making my stomach even worse. Luckily all of the food was vegetarian, which was great for us. We walked into this huge food hall, which was still inside the temple grounds. I guess you called call it that, it was basically a big empty room with long lines of mats on the floor, and a kitchen to one side.

We walked in and sat on the floor along the mats with everyone else. Before you know it some guy is coming up to us with a silver tray which was split into different sections, like the ones you see in the prison films where there's mash and some sort of meat slopped in it. Then they came and added different types of food to it. So like some bread, two kinds of curries some rice and some other little things, which I couldn't even explain if I wanted to. Lentil and bean based dishes. It was really nice, it was hard to enjoy a lot of the food in India, especially when you didn't know what it was, or how it was made. Just because you never knew if it was going to make you ill, or how your stomach would react. After a while my stomach got used to it, and I would eat most things quite happily, it was just the first few days in Delhi where I had to be careful.

Everything tasted great, they cleared away our plates, and came and gave us some pink water. They always used to offer this throughout India. I'm not sure what is was made of, but it was a deep pink and tasted like a sweet Pepto Bismal. I said no thank you, they were very persistent in giving us some, but I tried to explain how we cannot drink the tap water as it makes us ill, and that our body isn't use to it. They ended up giving us some anyway and saying something in broken English along the lines of it's hydrating. We took it anyway, just out of politeness, and we both left them on the mats, I think my Grandma may have drank hers, but I'm not 100% sue. The Sikh tuk tuk driver then proceeded to take us into the kitchen to show us where all the food was made.

This was really interesting, he took us around the back into the kitchen, and they had big vats of different styles of Indian food, most of them filled with curries of some sort. There were about 15 Indian women sat down making the thin bread, called chapati that they use to eat the curries with. He told us that they all do it for free, anyone can come in and help make it, none of it is paid for, they just come and help when they get time. They use the chapati as a spoon, they fold it in a specific way, and use it to kind of scoop up the curry and eat it. Many times I tried this and still by the end of the three week trip I ended up with curry all over my hands. I just couldn't get the hang of making a spoon from chapati.

After eating and looking around the kitchen, we left the temple, got back in the tuk tuk, and headed to the hostel. It was nearing 7pm, and weren't hungry as we had just eaten so there was no need for us to go out and get food. We got back to the hostel, did the usual and then chilled out for a bit. We then walked down to the local beer store and grabbed a couple of beers each. Beers were pretty cheap about 50p for a large bottle, so we picked up a couple of the local ones, then walked back to the hostel. For the rest of the night we just played cards, a couple other people from the hostel joined us, drank some beers and decided what we were going to do the next day.

Unfortunately this nights sleep was not the best for me.

I had to get up in the night a couple of times with some serious Delhi belly issues, it was painful, to make it worse, the toilets had no air-con or fans, so it was sweaty and hot, and you have belly ache, it was not a pleasant experience in the slightest.

After spending about 20 minutes in the toilet, I went back into the dorm room, dropped a couple of Imodium pills, and went to sleep. This was the third time I had been up and it was 2am in the morning, luckily that was the last time I was up.

Our first stop of the next day was the amazing Lotus Temple. This was built by a group of people who believe that worship is worship, no matter what religion one follows, and that all religions should worship together. They have members and Temples all over the world. Each Temple is pertinent to its own part of the world, hence the one in Delhi represents India's national flower, the Lotus. It's pure white, formed by a group of unsupported arched roots, smaller on the outside graduating to a large one in the middle, and is dazzling in the sunshine against the pure azure blue sky. Only so many are allowed in at one time so we had to wait our turn. Shoes are removed at the entrance and given into the safe keeping of an attendant. Each group has about twenty minutes inside for prayer, meditation or just to sit quietly and absorb the atmosphere. The lighting was soft and mellow and silence was the order of the day, so it was calm and peaceful. The only sound was the voices of the various ministers reading in turn from the holy books of all the world religions, no matter how small. I found it inspiring and uplifting to find Christianity, Islam, Judaism and so many more given equal importance in this one place.

Our next stop was the small room where Mahatma Gandhi spent the last 144 days of his life. This was totally different, with nothing in it but a bed one side with a kit bag, presumably containing bedding, resting on it and a rectangular seating divan and small table on the other. In a glass case in the hall were Ghandi Ji's (as the Indians call him) few simple tools and utensils, also his signature glasses. It was a very tranquil place, seeming to have absorbed Ghandi's philosophy of peace and harmony.

The Surrounding gardens were beautifully kept and the simple memorial stone in a gazebo at the side of Mahatma Gandhi's assassination and Martyrdom was a fitting tribute to him and his chosen lifestyle. Equally fitting was the site of Ghandi's grave. A plain square of block marble, the circles of dried orange marigold petals at each corner seemed to emphasise the austerity of the memorial. An eternal flame burns in a large square glass lantern at one side, and a small stone footstool, also covered with marigold petals, stands on the opposite side. Again, shoes had to removed at both holy sites, but cool green matting had been laid to protect the feet.

I found both sites as moving in a different way as the more grand Lotus Temple. Strangely it was outside the gates at Ghandi's home that we encountered our first street sellers of souvenirs.

Our last stop of the day was at Delhi's Sikh Temple. I have never seen a sight like it in my life! The white marble walls shone dazzling and the golden domes gleamed in the sun. Here Jake had to remove his socks as well as shoes and heads had to be covered. I used a fine pashmina I took especially for that purpose and Jake was given an orange triangle of cotton to tie around his head. Inside everything was covered in gold leaf.

All this magnificence was paid for by donations from the Sikh community. I just didn't know where to look first. To start with it seemed a sea of gold, but as our eyes adjusted details of the etched patterns on the walls started to emerge. After standing to marvel for a while we took our place in the line of people and filed in our turn past the priest (Is that what they are called?) to be blessed. Outside more marble gleamed and the large holy purification lake looked most inviting.

Unfortunately not being Sikh we were not permitted to try it. All Sikh temples have a large communal dining room attached where any member of the public could walk in and eat. For many of the poorer Indians this was their only meal of the day.

We were invited to try the food and, on accepting, collected an eating tray and took our seats cross-legged on the carpet strips laid out on the floor. The varied compartments of the tray were filled by servers bringing round large pans of food. Curry and rice, of course, but also chapati, vegetables and dips. It was extremely delicious and washed down with a very sweet pink drink. Jake was dubious about this as he thought that it had probably been made with local water, but I drank mine and suffered no ill effects. However I had not suffered from 'Delhi-belly' as poor Jake had!

The food was plentiful and, as was usual for most of the holiday, Jake had to finish mine. After the meal our guide offered to show us the kitchen. Again, Jake was dubious as he felt he didn't want to see the conditions and possible dirt when we had already eaten the food, but as I pointed out, would our guide be willing to show us if there was anything amiss. It was spotlessly clean! There were massive pots of various curries simmering away and volunteers were busy making chapatis, some by machine and some traditionally by hand. All the food is either bought by the Temple funds or donated, and the whole thing is run by volunteers.

This visit was a fitting end to what had been a marvellous day. We had hired our driver from 10:30am to 4:30 pm but it was nearer to 6 o'clock when he took us back to our hostel. Also, he had gone beyond our expectations, so we felt he had earned an extra 100 rupee's, and we parted on the most cordial terms.

Chapter 6 – Day 4 New Delhi

We woke at around 8am for our last day in New Delhi, and headed down for breakfast, after doing the usual stuff of showering, getting dressed, sun creaming up and packing my backpack for the day, we met downstairs. We had to book our train to Jaipur this morning, so we spoke to the guy at the hostel reception and he said he could book us onto a train, which made things super easy as saved us going all the way to the train station.

The train was pretty cheap costing about £5 each for a 4 hour journey. This train would take us further south, so it would get even hotter, going from New Delhi early in the morning to Jaipur arriving about 11am. After booking our train and booking our hostel for Jaipur, we ate breakfast, and today we had decided to go to the New Delhi zoo. It was about 11am by the time we left the hostel, after booking everything for Jaipur and getting breakfast.

Once outside the sun was already baking hot, and after walking down the road for about 20 minutes, I noticed I had forgotten my sunglasses…. Again. My Grandma laughed a little at me, as for the fourth day running, I had forgotten my sunglasses. As she said 'it was supposed to be her that was beginning to forget stuff not me'. She asked me if I wanted to go back but I thought it was too late, and decided not to considering it was already nearly 11.30. We got into a tuk tuk, negotiated a price, after about 10 minutes, and walking away from the driver twice, he finally yelled back at us 'okay okay', and agreed to our price. We jumped in and headed to the zoo.

After about 25 minutes I began to worry, where the hell are we going the zoo was supposed to be a 15 minute ride away. I looked at my Grandma and decided we should say something so he knew he was going to the right place. I tapped him on his shoulder and said in the easiest way possible to help him understand 'you know where you're going', to the zoo?

He looked at me confused, and all I thought was, oh for fuck sake, this is going to be a nightmare.

I grabbed my map out of my bag, and pointed at where we wanted to go, he said 'okay okay', I know', he didn't speak a lot of English at all, which made it even more difficult to try and tell him, where we wanted to go. After about 15 more minutes of driving. I tapped him on the shoulder again and asked him to pull over.

I got out the map again and pointed and said, 'we want to go here, to the zoo, do you know where you're going'. He got out of his tuk tuk and went and asked a group of tuk tuk drivers who were sat around drinking and smoking, they seemed to know where it was and explained the route to him. He got back into the tuk tuk and said 'I know, I know'. We both looked at each other and said why would he agree to take us, if he had no clue at all where it was.

After another 10 minutes of driving we arrived at the zoo, going in the complete opposite direction to what we had come. We got out the tuk tuk and gave him the amount we agreed to. Which I knew would be an issue.

He wasn't happy with this at all and complained saying about how long he was driving for and that he wanted more. I just politely said to him, no it was your fault, you got lost not us and said that is the price we agreed to. We then just walked away and headed to the entrance of the zoo, we could still hear him shouting and complaining, but we just continued to walk and didn't look back.

Once we got to the zoo entrance, there were two entrances, one for women and one for men, so me and my Grandma both proceeded to our respective entrances and said we would wait for each other the other side. We both went up to the gates, and paid for our tickets, they also charged you extra if you had a camera. I tried as best as I could to hide mine, but they still found it. They didn't however find my Grandmas, so she was happy about that.

Once I was inside, I waited about 10 more minutes and my Grandma came through the other side, we both grabbed some water, and walked towards the map, so we could see where we wanted to go.

It was much much hotter than the previous days, it was around 40C, and unfortunately for us, there was very little shade throughout the zoo, so we were in direct sunlight all day. To make matters worse, I had a serious case of Delhi belly going on today, literally every 10-15 minutes I felt like I needed to be running to the toilet. This was really not what I wanted in the middle of a zoo, in 40C heat.

We continued to walk around the zoo, after looking at the map, we had a rough idea of what we wanted to see. The main reason for us coming to the zoo, was to see the white tigers. They looked really beautiful and they can't be seen from many places in the world, so we thought we would take the opportunity to go and see them.

We walked around the zoo and saw a range of animals. Then we decided to head to the white tiger enclosure. It seemed that the white tigers were locked away around the back, maybe for feeding, or for the zoo keepers to clean the enclosures, we were not sure but we were pretty gutted as that's the main reason we came to the zoo in the first place.

We continued to walk through the zoo, and everyone we met seemed to want a picture with us, which we found quite amusing. So many Indian men and women would come walking up to me and my Grandma, and asked if they could take a picture with us. I guess they didn't see many white people walking around the zoo, literally nearly everyone was asking for a picture, it was okay at the start but after about 20-30 people it got a little boring. I mean, we were just here to enjoy the zoo.

We continued to walk around the zoo, and all of a sudden I felt the desperate urge that I needed to go to the toilet. I had a really bad stomach all day, but this was bad, sorry for the horrible image, but it felt like my stomach was about to explode, god damn my inquisitiveness to try new foods. As good as they tasted, they did dangerous things to my stomach.

I said to my Grandma that I needed to go to the toilet, so we walked and tried to find the closest one. Luckily the zoo had toilets, or I would have 100% been squatting in the nearest enclosure with any bush cover.

After 10 minutes of walking and my intestines doing knots in my stomach, we finally found some toilets. I walked in as quickly as I could, there was only one toilet in the building, luckily it wasn't locked.

I opened the door and never expected it, but

then who would, to my unfortunate surprise...

Someone had shit on the seat..

Not in the toilet..

Not even on the floor..

But on the actual toilet seat.

Oh for god sake I thought, I literally couldn't wait any longer, I only had one choice... to clean it up.

There was no toilet roll in the toilet… But luckily I always carried some in my bag, just in case of emergencies like this one.

I loaded it into my hand so it was about 50 sheets thick and wiped this stinking shit of the seat. I cleaned it up, covered the seat in about 5 layers of toilet roll and sat down. Did my business and left. To make matters worse the toilet was hot, sticky and smelly, so I'll leave it to your imagination as to how I felt.

About twenty minutes later, I came out of the toilet, covered my hands and my arms all the way up to my elbows in hand sanitiser, and told my Grandma what the toilet was like. I don't know whether she was joking, or being serious, but she said, 'I'm glad I don't have Delhi belly'. We both just laughed.

We continued to walk around the zoo, and to our joy the white tigers were now in the enclosure, we watched them for about 20 minutes, walking and eating, they were really beautiful animals. We were both super happy we got to see them, especially seeing as that was the main reason why we went to the zoo in the first place.

We walked to the next kiosk that sold food and drink, and both got a mango juice, I kid you not this stuff was incredible, especially when it was hot, and the juice was cold. I think we both had at least two a day. Neither of us were very hungry at this point, me because I don't think my stomach could take it, and my Grandma just said she wasn't. I think as mentioned before, that the hot weather and humidity makes you less hungry, which is kind of surprising.

After finishing the mango juices, we headed to the exit of the zoo, a few more photos with local

Indians and a toilet break, we left and headed to the nearest tuk tuk. To be honest I was just ready to get back to the hostel, get a shower, and relax for a little bit. Particularly since my stomach was in bits. It was only about 3pm, but after haggling with a tuk tuk driver and the drive back, it was about 3.45pm. We got to the hostel, and just chilled. I was on my phone a little, caught up with emails and Skyped a few friends, and my Grandma was happily reading her book. After a couple of hours it was about 7-7.30 in the evening and we decided to order some food to the hostel.

It was pretty cool, the hostel we were staying in called Joey's had loads of menus on the tables, and if you wanted any food delivering to the hostel, you just decided what you want, told the guy at the reception and he would call and place your order for you.

We both decided to order the same thing, we ordered this dish called palak paneer, it was like a green spinach dish, with lumps of cheese called panecr in it, and we also ordered a few garlic chapatis. It was amazing, it was nothing too spicy that would upset my stomach, and it was definitely my new favourite dish. We both loved it and finished it all off.

After eating, and talking to a few people in the hostel, we decided to get an early night as we had to be up at 6am to get our first Indian train to Jaipur, where we would spend 2 nights. So we said our good nights and headed up to pack our bags and get some sleep. I went to bed praying that my stomach would be better the following day. The last thing I wanted was a dodgy stomach on the train. Even more so as I had no idea what to expect from the train journey or train itself.

Our last day in Delhi was spent at the zoo. Jake really wanted to see the white tigers he had heard so much about. After paying the modest entry fee (although it was twice as much as the Indians paid) and having our bags checked for plastic bags (I don't know why) we headed off towards the enclosures.

We saw some deer, and then some more deer. We saw monkeys by the dozen, many with babies, strolling down the paths and rummaging in the bins for discarded food, and then we saw some more deer! We saw rhinos, and Indian and an African elephant, and more deer! Then, tigers at last, however they were Bengal tigers. Magnificent creatures, lying in the shade or cooling off in the water. But they weren't white tigers.

Eventually we saw one! Sitting inside a large shed-like structure, we could see it through a small mesh covered window. He has his back to us as if he were sulking.

Jake was a bit disappointed, but philosophical, saying that at least he had seen one! We walked on round the corner looking for the exit and a few yards down the path, lo and behold, a large enclosure full of white tigers! Well, there were about eight or so, and that many tigers can do quite a lot of filling. Some were resting in the shade, some were patrolling the enclosure and one was keeping cool in the water. Jake was so excited and we spent at least another half an hour just watching them and taking the odd photo. Seeing these magnificent creatures was the highlight of our day.

That night it was an early night for us as we had to be up bright and early the next morning to catch the train to our next destination Jaipur.

Chapter 7 – Day 1 Jaipur

We awoke at about 5.30, grabbed showers, got dressed and got our backpacks, leaving Joey's at about 5.55. We went outside, grabbed a tuk tuk and headed to the train station. It took us about 25 minutes to get to the train station, we already had our tickets, and our train was at 7am, we wanted to arrive with plenty of time to spare, just in case. We got to the train station and walked into the main entrance, it was pretty busy inside, lots of people rushing around and queuing to buy train tickets. We looked up at the big screen and it was full of train numbers and times. We just matched that with what it said on our ticket, and went to the platform that the screen indicated us to go to.

It was much easier than I thought it was going to be, we got to the platform, it was pretty much like getting a train in any modern city, the train pulled up about 5 minutes early, so we got on, found our seats, and got comfy. Again to my surprise, the train was actually pretty nice, the seats were comfy and reclined, it was air conditioned and there was plenty of room, not like what I had read or heard about trains in India. We got comfy and both looked out the window as we headed for Jaipur and left the big city of New Delhi, and hopefully leaving my Delhi belly there to.

Passing through the outskirts of Delhi was also an experience, lots of strange and saddening things to see as the train passed through. It really was an eye opener and nothing like central Delhi. There were lots of children walking around along side of the train tracks. Houses made just of wood and large plastic sheets, as well as animals wandering on the edge of the train tracks. It continued for miles and miles. Just miles and miles of shabby built houses made of wood and plastic sheets, it really makes you appreciative of the life we were just luckily born into.

About an hour into the train ride, the train staff came around with a tray. Which had a teapot, a biscuit, and some condiments on it. Me and my Grandma both looked at each other in surprise. All i was thinking was this is amazing, a free breakfast on the train, perfect. I knew it wouldn't be eggs and bacon or even coco pops, but food was food at 8am when you were starving. After about another 10 minutes they came around with the actual food, and a pot of hot water, presumably for the tea. Sweet! It was actually really nice and was all vegetarian, which was perfect. There was some sort of curry/rice dish which was pretty nice and some sort of crispy cylindrical samosa (Like a masala flavoured spring roll). All of it was really nice, and the cup of tea just topped it off. After eating and finishing our cups of tea, which absolutely hit the spot, they cleared everything up. I then stuck in my headphones and decided to get a couple hours sleep, and my Grandma opened up her book.

I closed my eyes and kept sleeping on an off for the next couple of hours, my Grandma was still reading her book quite happily. I got up and went to the toilet, another hole in the ground toilet, but this one was different, as you could see the train tracks passing underneath as you look where the toilet was supposed to be. I just kind of stood, lent backwards and did my business. The toilet was literally just like a hole in the bottom of the train, it was a little sketchy watching the train tracks pass underneath while I went to the toilet. I could imagine having to squat over it would create even more unease.

I went back to my seat, washed my hands using

hand sanitiser, as I don't think I ever saw soap or hand wash in a toilet in India, other than in the hostels.

There were about 15 minutes of our first train journey left until we arrived in Jaipur, so I packed up my few bits, and me and my Grandma just spoke about what we were going to do for the rest of the day as we pulled into the station. It was 11am as we arrived and we still had to find the hostel, as we arrived in Jaipur we grabbed our bags and jumped off the train.

Jaipur wasn't the last stop, there were many stops afterwards, it was going far down south India, so we had to be sure we didn't miss Jaipur. We managed to get of at the right stop, and as soon as we stepped of the train, we were bombarded by taxi and tuk tuk drivers, trying to get our custom. We just continued to walk past them, of the train platform and out of the station. At first I thought we should just walk to the hostel as it said 25 minutes on google maps, so we walked down the street, and came to a busy intersection I had a look at my maps and a look at the road. Already I was lost and literally had no idea how to get to the hostel, I looked at my Grandma and just said shall we get a tuk

tuk, she looked at the map and couldn't figure out which road we had to take either.

It was approaching midday, so the temperature was really starting to pick up, and we were both sweating like crazy despite only being outside for 15 minutes, so we decided to get a tuk tuk. We walked back towards the station where there were loads of tuk tuk's and asked the first one, he gave us some absurd price, it was at most a 10 minute journey and he said 1200 rupees, at first I though he was joking, but he was being deadly serious, we both just looked at each other in astonishment and continued to walk down towards the station. After haggling and chatting to about 4 different tuk tuk drivers we finally got one down to 400 rupees, which was 200 each, and we were happy to pay it. We got in, it was a fairly youngish guy and he drove us to the hostel, he did get a little lost, but he soon asked around and we soon found it. I think the 10 minute journey took us in total 20 minutes, because he got a little lost, but it didn't really matter.

By the time we got to the hostel it was about midday, which was perfect as it was roasting hot, we got checked in and both went to our rooms, and said we would meet in the lounge area of the hostel at 12.30. I went up to the room, got all my stuff sorted out, repacked my bag and slapped on a load more sun cream. Everyone was out of the room, obviously as it was midday and I guess they were all out exploring. The hostel was pretty quiet anyway, as it was summer, and the majority of people went up north India in the summer where it is cooler, rather than down to the south where it's hotter. The hostel was nice, it was clean, had a pool table and lots of nice areas to chill out in, we were pretty happy with it.

We met back downstairs at 12.30 and said we would just go for a wander around the pink city and have a look for a few hours to see what Jaipur had to offer. We also decided we would go and buy me a new adaptor as Grandma accidentally left our other one in the hostel. She only had an old phone, and she didn't use it very often, so she only really had to charge her phone once every 3-4 days. Unlike me who had to charge it everyday, and literally used it for everything, from booking hostels, to seeing what there was we could do. Grandma had totally forgot about it and left it in the wall in the last hostel, so she said she would get a new one for us to use.

We grabbed our bags and left the hostel, right outside was an electric store which was perfect, we went and told him we needed an adaptor, and he pulled us one out, I just checked to see if it worked and it did, and it was only 100 rupees which I thought was a good price. So I ran back inside the hostel, stuck my phone on charge and it would hopefully be charged by the time we got back from exploring.

We walked a little down the side road which the hostel was situated on and went to look for a tuk tuk to take us into the pink city. At the end of the street there were about 3-4 tuk tuks waiting. We found that almost every time we needed a tuk tuk, there would be a few at the end of the street. We negotiated a price, as you always do when in India, and were then on our way to see the pink city.

It was sweltering in the back of this tuk tuk, I think it was the hottest, in fact it was definitely the hottest temperature I had ever been in, it was about 45c at midday, my legs were sticking to the leather tuk tuk seats, and I was wiping the sweat of my fore head every ten seconds. My

Grandma doing the same, we got through so many bottles of water it was ridiculous. The ride took us about 20 minutes. We shot down little back alleys of the pink city, as he took us towards the centre, the dust flicking up from the small wheels of the tuk tuk. Both me and my Grandma having to pull our caps over our heads to stop the sand and dirt from getting into our eyes, and also covering our faces, the dust mixing with the already nice combination of sweat and sun cream.

We finally got to the centre of the pink city as the tuk tuk pulled up outside a busy area, and he said to us 'here my friend'. We stepped out of the side of the tuk tuk, and as soon as my feet touched the ground I could feel the intense heat of the midday Indian summer sun beating down onto my body. I paid the driver and he shot off, sounding his horn while simultaneously looking for his next customer. We both wiped down our foreheads for the 50th time that hour, and started to have a look around this incredible city.

It was already about 2.30 in the afternoon, so we decided not too do too much and just have a wander, we thought we would save most of it for the day after, rather than rush through it all in a few hours.

The pink city was really beautiful. As you can imagine, beautiful pink walls, with decoration and painting on them, the décor on some of the walls was incredible. Some of the walls were slightly faded, I guess from the many years of sandy winds. I cant begin to imagine how beautiful it must have looked all those years ago when it was thriving with energy and life.

The one thing we did want to see today was something called the Hawa Mahal, this was the front of a palace. It's a 5 story screen which is incredibly decorated, it seemed more so than the rest of the pink city. History says this is where the women of the royal family would watch the parades and festivities below, they would watch them up here from above so they could not be seen, and would watch through the small windows of the palace.

We were just randomly wandering wherever our feet took us and down whatever side streets looked the most interesting. After about another hour of just aimlessly wandering, we decided we just really wanted to get to Hawa Mahal now. So we began to ask the locals for directions to Hawa Mahal. Being as it is the most famous part of Jaipur, we thought most of the locals would know where it was and it would be an easy task to get someone to point us in the right direction. We were clearly mistaken. For some reason we were getting nowhere and most people just seemed to shake there heads, or just seemed confused by what we were saying, and in their friendly manner just pointed anywhere.

So to google maps it was. I flicked through the maps a little bit and managed to locate which street the Hawa Mahal was on, and in which direction we needed to walk. Turns out somehow, and so my Grandma would tell you, we would always end up in some back alley area of India, a little of the tourist path where all the local trades seemed to take place. Luckily we weren't that far away from Hawa Mahal, just a 10 minute walk, so of we headed and before we knew it, it was right in front of us.

It really was beautiful, we stood and admired it for a few minutes, and then decided to get some pictures, we then asked a local shop owner if he could take a picture of us both together, of course he gladly did, but not without inviting us into his shop to see all his 'very cheap, very good' gifts. We kindly said thank you, and decided not to go into his shop, and instead head of and try to find a place to get another drink. Preferably a cold one, and even more preferably one of our favourites, a mango juice.

We continued to look around for a place to grab a drink, we were both super thirsty by this point and there seemed nothing around, we had been looking for a shop that sold cold drinks for a good 20 minutes now, until we decided to say hell with it, lets head back to the hostel.

It was about 4pm, 4.30pm by the time we got back to the hostel, and it was showing no signs of cooling down. As soon as we got out of the tuk tuk, we darted across the road to the local little shop and grabbed two large cold mango juices, we drank them as we walked backed to the hostel. When you've been drinking warm water for the past 4 hours, and it's been +40c, anything cold and fruity touching the back of your throat is heaven.

I soon drank mine, Grandma savoured hers and drank it over the course of thirty minutes. I was incredibly tempted to go and get another one.

We sat and just chilled in the air conditioned room for a while, I caught up on messages and emails on my phone and Grandma read some of her book. We then decided we would both go and get showers, freshen up, and go grab a couple beers.

About 30 minutes later, we re-grouped downstairs. We asked the guy on the front desk where we could get some beers, and he gave us directions. I was just trying to remember which streets we had to go left and right down, but between us we managed. We decided we would just order food again. There didn't really seem a lot of choice in regards to restaurants around, and we were both happy with sipping a couple of beers, playing cards, and having the food delivered to us. We were both knackered too, so it sounded like the perfect plan to the both of us.

After walking for about 10 minutes we found a liquor store, grabbed two large beers each, we both agreed there wasn't much point getting small ones when it was 20p more to get a large. By the time we got back to the hostel we were both starving, understandably so seen as we hadn't eaten since breakfast other than a packet of crisps each. We grabbed a menu and of course, we'd have no chance of ordering ourselves food. So we asked the receptionist to order for us, after our order was placed, both our stomachs were grumbling even more. At least we both had beer till the food came, which to make even better had been sitting in the fridge. So we cracked two cold ones open, and said cheers to another incredible day exploring India together while we waited for our food to come.

After thirty minutes, which seemed more like 30 hours, our food arrived. I went and grabbed it, paid the guy what was like £3 and took it back to the chill out area of the hostel. The hostel was still empty. I think there were only around 5 people checked in.

The food smelt amazing, we ordered chapatis, palak paneer.. one of our favourites, some bhajis, and another vegetable curry dish, I can't remember the name of it, but it was kind of a creamy tomato dish. It was all amazing, maybe due to the fact we were both so hungry, but it went down incredibly well. Clearing out the silver tins in which it came so there wasn't scrap of food left. We both had another beer, played some more cards and then headed to bed at about 9.30-10pm.

Surprisingly this was my choice as I was so tired. I'm sure Grandma would've been keen to stay up for another beer and some more cards, but I was knackered and I could barely even keep my eyes open. So to bed we both went.

The train to Jaipur was a real eye-opener. For a few rupee's we boarded a comfortable air-conditioned train and were presented with a pot of tea and a large bottle of water. However, this was not the end of it. Once we got going breakfast was the order of the day. Juice, spicy sausages, curry, naan bread, fruit and more tea. All this included in the fare of about £3. The trains are understandably packed and extremely successful. British Rail – take note!

On arrival in Jaipur we took the inevitable tuk-tuk to our hostel and after settling in we set off to explore. Jaipur's more notable landmark is the Pink City. This does what it says on the tin. It's a massive area of impressive rose-pink buildings, housing, shops, offices and residences. It's an amazing sight glowing softly in the sunshine, set off by stripes and accents in mellow cream. It had it's smelly corners, of course, as all Indian cities do, but it is a really beautiful place.

Chapter 8 – Day 2 Jaipur

Today we decided to meet at about 9. So after doing the usual, shower and get sweaty 10 seconds after drying ourselves, cover ourselves in sun cream and get dressed already feeling sticky, we were ready for our second day in hottest city on the earth, not literally, but what felt like it at the time.

Today we were unsure what we were going to do, we wanted to go see this floating temple and also visit some of the markets. So we just thought we would have a wander, get a tuk tuk and go see the floating temple first. So as we did the previous day we wandered down the road to where all the tuk tuk were usually parked... and there were no tuk tuks. So we decided to just walk down the road until someone honked their horn at us.

It didn't take long before tuk tuk drivers were fighting over who saw us first, we just jumped into the closest one to us. We told him, we wanted to go see the floating temple, and some of the markets, he said he would show us around and drive us about for part of the day so we came to an agreed price, which seemed fair.

Especially considering we didn't have to look for tuk tuk drivers at every place we got out at, as he was going to take us around for a few hours.

First stop was the floating temple. Now I thought this would be really cool, apparently it was a restaurant, and as you can gather from the name, a temple floating on one of the lakes of Jaipur. We turned up and to be quite honest it wasn't that great at all. There was all rubbish lying around the outside of the lake and on the pavements, and the temple itself was nothing impressive. It looked really amazing in the pictures we looked at on google. Maybe this was due to the fact that we had seen some amazing temples in New Delhi, as well as the incredible pink city, it just didn't live up to the standards we set it. After getting out of the tuk tuk for a few brief seconds, we had a walk up and down, and decided we had seen enough.

Much to the drivers surprise that we were done already, we left and said we wanted to go to the markets next, and he said he had some 'special very good market' to show us. Now the market we planned on going to was a small local market, in which the people sold all kinds of goods they had made themselves. We had a funny feeling this wasn't the market he planned on taking us to. Me and my Grandma just looked at each other, it seemed that we had this way of saying yes, no or what's going on, without actually saying anything. Just with a simple look we knew what we meant, but this time we decided to go with it, because after all, we were here to go on an adventure. After agreeing and speeding of in the tuk tuk we decided to see how 'very special good' this market was.

After driving down the back alleys of Jaipur and exchanging a few more of those looks, he pulled up to a few rows of buildings and said this was the market. It didn't really look like a market, more like a row of shops, but we decided to take a look anyway, he said he would wait parked outside for us. In my head I was thinking I bloody hope so, because I haven't seen a person, or a car drive past in the five minutes since we've been here.

We began walking along the row of shops, but nothing seemed to take our fancy most of them were fabric shops, and there were quite a few shops closed. Turns out it wasn't a special very good market after all. We did have a look in a few of the clothing shops, because we were were looking for harem pants, but they were all pretty expensive, well for India standards anyway. We continued walking around, it had now been about 20 minutes, and we found a tea shop. My Grandma really wanted to buy some tea from India as gifts, and for herself as she is a big tea fan. In fact, every time I go to her house I have to look through about 7 different tins just to find a normal tea bag, just because of the assortment of different flavoured teas she has.

So we entered the shop to find a young man waiting behind the counter, he only seemed to be around my age, which was 20 at the time. He greeted us, and spoke perfect English, after talking for a little while we found out that we went to university in London. He said he really enjoyed it and would love to come back to live and work, but he couldn't get the visa, so for the time being he was running his own tea and spice shop. We were sat on these little stools in front of the counter, and he brought us out a range of tea to smell. He gave us prices for different styles and also gave us the benefits to drinking the different teas, and how different types benefited your health. I mean I'm not sure how accurate all of it was, but it was really interesting to listen to. After about 15 minutes of him showing us different teas, my Grandma decided on a few she liked, and passed the bartering over to me. We haggled back and forth for 5 minutes until we got a reasonable price which they were both happy with. We paid, said our goodbyes and wished him good luck with his future as we left the shop.

We walked a little further down the road, looking in some gift and souvenir shops but nothing took our fancy. We walked all the way back down the road until we got back to the tuk tuk, luckily he was still there. I mean I'm pretty sure he wasn't going anywhere, mainly due to the fact we hadn't paid him yet. But we still would've been stuck if he'd left.

Once back in the tuk tuk the driver said he had a surprise to show us, as he said 'something really cool'. Again we both exchanged a look, but both of us having adventurous souls couldn't pass up the opportunity for a surprise, so we agreed. I was just hoping it wasn't another 'market'.

After driving and again shooting through the

back lanes of Jaipur in this little tuk tuk, which was really quite and experience. The little lanes in some cases no longer than a meter and a half wide and the pink walls high up either side were quite beautiful. There were local people walking down the street who had to jump out of the way of the tuk tuk, as well as dogs and on occasion a chicken or a cow we had to pull over for. We pulled up against part of this old wall, and he said 'here'. We looked around and it didn't seem that there was much 'here' to be seen. We got out of the tuk tuk all be it reluctantly and followed him around a corner into this big style courtyard. Which as we turned there were two elephants inside, it really was quite a shock. When I turned the corner I was expecting someone to be selling me something not two elephants to be stood, eating and strolling around the courtyard. After spending a few minutes here we then decided to leave, the young guy who I am guessing owned or at least looked after these elephants asked us for a tip, which I quite frankly was not willing to give. So I politely said we had no change, he understood, shook our hands and off we walked back to the tuk tuk.

The driver seemed incredibly please with

himself because of what he showed us, so we showed our gratitude, even though I thought it was harsh on the elephants.

We said we would like to be dropped of at the city palace, which was big museum consisting of several parts, and something that sounded quite interesting. We also thought we would get some lunch as it was about 1pm.

Neither of us were really that hungry, but we thought we should definitely eat something, as we hadn't eaten all day. It was just with the heat, neither of us really ever had an appetite. We found a small little local place and just decided to share a plate of vegetable noodles. I cant specifically remember what the name for it was, or what it said on the menu, but I knew what it meant at the time. It came to around £2 for a big plate of vegetable noodles and two cokes, we were both full even after sharing. It would definitely do us until we ordered our takeaway again later than evening, which we had already decided would be a good idea rather than go on the lookout for a restaurant, as there really wasn't a lot going on within the vicinity of the hostel.

After eating we headed to the city palace. Much to my Grandmas disappointment, there was a discount for students and Indians but not for OAP's. She really wasn't happy about this, as it meant I got in at half the price, and it really was quite expensive for foreigners to enter. I said it was up to her and she could decide, and she decided we might as well. It was only a few pound, and as she put it, we were only here once.

We went to the ticket office, and bought our tickets, me buying mine with a smile, and Grandma buying hers with a frown, no I'm joking but I do think she was a little bit annoyed with the price difference. After being issued our tickets and grabbing a map we headed into the city palace, and what a sight it was. Beautifully decorated walls 3-4 stories high, with glistening turrets on the top, and different coloured decoration on each section of the palace. The museum was split up into different sections for different parts of Indian history, such as weapons, family life, fabrics, etc.

We wandered around the museum for a couple of hours, looking at all the different sections and learning about the Indian history. We were now sweating so much, since we had been walking around in the heat of the day for a good couple of hours. As we walked we wandered past a restaurant which look expensive and we both immediately thought... air-con. A waiter came over to us to see if we wanted a seat, we politely said no, and just pretended to examine the expensive menu, savouring every second we could in this air-conditioned room. After standing in there for around 5 minutes, we decided it was probably time to leave and face the heat again.

So we left the restaurant, and headed back outside into the palace grounds. There was a big roof covered area, made from stone. It had a big marble patio with four pillars in each corner. The stone roof, of course pink, was all beautifully decorated with delicate paintwork of a light brown colour. Seated inside this covered area were loads of artists, which were all painting the surrounding palace. We stood and watched for 15 minutes, some of the paintings were beautiful. I mean the young people painting them really were talented, some of them being as young as 4 or 5. After watching for a little while we decided we were pretty much done in the museum. We had looked around all of the different sections, learnt about different weapons used, got to see how the people of Jaipur lived, and got an insight into what family life was like those years ago. It was a really interesting museum.

We left the museum after a few hours of wandering around, and of course grabbed a cold mango juice and a couple bags of crisps form the small store across the road. We then got a tuk tuk back to the hostel.

It was around 4.30, so we both just chilled for an hour. Grandma read her book and checked the messages on her phone and I browsed through social media a little bit, caught up with everyone, and had a look at how we could get a train to Agra, and also what to do the next day.

After an hour or so, we decided to go for a shower to get rid of the days sweaty sun cream layer on our skin, and then we would head out, grab some beers and order food. After walking to the liquor store and Grandma yet again persuading me to get two large beers each not just one, we headed back and ordered the same food as the night before since it tasted so amazing. We drank our beers, played some cards, and ate amazing Indian food. I was pretty happy we got two large beers about an hour later and very grateful for the persuasion of my Grandma, not that I took much persuading at all.

We continued drinking beers and playing cards until about 10:30pm and then headed up to bed, we decided we were going to get up early the next day and get the train to Agra, home of the Taj Mahal. It was about 3 hours away by train, so we wanted to get to the station early to book our tickets and then we could spend the afternoon exploring, and arrive in Agra for the evening. So off to bed we went, ready to be up early so we could book our train to Agra, and enjoy our final day in Jaipur.

As in Delhi, we hired a tuk-tuk to give us a tour, but this time only for a couple of hours. We were taken to an elephant house and were introduced to the elephants and their keeper. They were magnificent beasts, I felt a bit sorry for them. We declined the offer of an elephant ride so our guide took us to a small complex of shops, hoping for better luck. The largest shop sold silks, wall hangings and leather goods. We were taken upstairs, plied with the inevitable tea and shown an amazing array of silk goods from quilts of all sizes and prices to beautiful slippers and bags. We could also have had a tunic made in about 2 hours. However, we resisted all the shopkeepers blandishments, much to his disappointment.

We were then taken into the tea and spice shop, where our senses were assailed by the rich aromas of Indian spices. We tried more tea (of course) and had many different spices demonstrated in an effort to get us to part with our rupee's. Jake held firm, but, feeling sorry for the poor shopkeeper, I did buy a small bag of spices to take home as a gift for my son-in-law. Later experience taught me that I could have got it much cheaper in the market in Delhi.

Our guide then decided he was going to pass us onto a friend to take us back to the hostel. However, he wanted us to pay him for the tour and his friend for the lift back to the city centre. Jake made it abundantly clear that that was not going to happen. Eventually, after a much spirited discussion, we were returned safely to our point of departure at no extra cost to us.

Another beautiful place was the People's Museum, housed in the Original Maharajah's Palace. Jake was able to get in at student rate, but I had no such luck. As a 'rich' tourist I had to pay the full whack – of about £2! In contrast to the Pink City a lot of the museum was made of yellow sandstone, mellowed over time to a rich clotted cream. Once again we were not allowed to take photos inside the exhibition building. These two halls housed an amazing collection of armour and weapons in one, and gorgeous, opulent fabrics in the other. Housed in an open mews were the sumptuous carriages and ornate howdah's used by the Maharaja's for centuries.

It was here that I found the spirit of his grandad was alive and kicking in Jake. They both love exploring where they shouldn't! We found a little door hidden in a corner and through it we could see a staircase. Hoping it would take us up to the flat roof we ventured in. We were right, but when we got up there we found building materials scattered around and workmen busy on one side. It was made clear to us that we were to go back down, which we did with apologies, but not before we had a panoramic view of the buildings and courtyards below us.

Chapter 9 – Day 3 Jaipur/Day 1 Agra

Today we woke up reasonably early around 7am and were ready to head out exploring by about 8. Today we were going to Agra, we decided we were going to get a train to Agra at about midday, which would then arrive into Agra for about 4pm. This meant we could get an early night and wake up early to see the Taj Mahal at sunrise. We were both super excited to get to Agra and see the Taj Mahal, it was one of the main reasons my Grandma decided to come to India, ticking it of her bucket list.

We were up early, our bags packed, showered and checked out of the hostel by 8am. Today we decided to head to the Amber fort and palace, it was about 25 minutes tuk tuk ride from the hostel, but definitely worth the ride. A beautiful fort situated on the mountainside of India. We headed for around 30 minutes along dusty roads, riding through the Indian countryside, and arrived at the Amber fort for around 8.30. We had made the decision to leave at about 11am giving us an hour to get back to the hostel and get showered again. I knew we'd be covered in sweat and wouldn't want to be sitting on the train for four hours feeling disgusting.

And then that would give us time to get to the
train station without rushing and ensure we
made the 12pm to Agra.

The closer we got to Amer which is the small
town where the fort is located, the more we
could see the fort rising from within the
mountains, and the more impressive it became.
The same as the pink city in Jaipur, the fort was
constructed out of this red/pink coloured stone,
built high with turrets and incredible decoration.
The perfectly clear blue Indian summer sky
behind it, it almost did glisten on the
mountainside. The tuk tuk driver pulled up at
the bottom and said he could wait for us and
take us back, that sounded perfect to us so we
agreed to two hours and a price, and he offered
to wait and take us back to the hostel. We
decided we would walk up into to the palace,
we were told it would take about 30 minutes to
reach the top which we didn't mind. Especially
since the only other way up was by truck, which
of course they charged tourists extortionate
amounts for.

We started our accent up the hillside towards
the entrance of the fort. It was beautiful,
perfectly preserved green gardens with all sorts

of flowers and plants, even in the heat of the summer. When up close you really could see the amount of effort and the attention to detail that went into decorating the palace, each painting telling its own story.

When we got to the top we looked outwards across the small town of Amer, what a breathtaking view. For miles you see the small brick red houses and the tuk tuks flying around below. It felt peaceful, looking down on the hectic Indian streets from up at the top. We stood and admired the view from the top, and the peacefulness for about 30 minutes before we started our descent. We had been walking down for about 10 minutes and decided to take a rest, and also enjoy the view a little more. There was a small brick wall which was just below waist height and made the perfect bench, so we took a seat and again looked out admiring the beautiful views from the top of the fort. Me and Grandma were both just sat there in our own little worlds just letting out minds wander, and also envisioning how awesome seeing the Taj Mahal tomorrow was going to be. Not uttering a word, just staring into the distant countryside. Until a small Indian girl taps me on the shoulder and says 'photo'. At first I just thought she just wanted me to take a photo of her and her family at the palace, but I turned out to be wrong. She wanted a picture with us, now we had both experienced this before in Delhi with the locals wanting to take pictures with us, but this one girl seemed to start a train of people wanting photos, it was quite ridiculous, while also amusing.

We politely said yes, and they took it in turns and had a family photo with us and left, but as they left another group of girls saw them having pictures with us, and I guess thought they would seize the opportunity. They came running up and asked for a photo, this continued to happen for about 5 groups of people, until me and Grandma had decided we were tired of being celebrities already, and made a dash for it back down the hillside.

We walked briskly for about 10 minutes until we had escaped the attention of the locals, and wandered back down the hillside of the palace. There was a market down this one side of the palace, so we headed towards it. We stopped and looked at all the items they had on offer, it was the usual touristy stuff, from ornaments and hand crafted wooden items, as well as the usual herbs, spices and tea leaves. After walking through the market and taking the occasional stop to see what they were selling, we found our way back down to the bottom of the palace. It really was quite beautiful. The peaceful gardens with all different flowers and trees, and the occasional pond, which was ridiculously tempting to get in. As well as a few random donkeys wandering around. All was so peaceful until someone would pester us for a ride back into the city in their tuk tuk.

We got back to the bottom and it was only 10am so we thought we would grab one of those mango juices I've mentioned so many times. We drank our thirst quenching mango juice and headed back to where the tuk tuk was parked. We jumped in and headed back to the hostel ready for our train to Agra. After another bumpy tuk tuk ride, we arrived back at the hostel at around 10.45, he seemed a lot quicker on the way back, not that there were any speed limits, but he seemed to be going a lot faster. I had used tuk tuks before in Thailand and Vietnam and loved them. They were cheap, fast and could usually weave there way in and out of any traffic that was in the way. When in Delhi we saw one overturned on its side, to be honest no wonder at the speed they take some corners. I've seen numerous tuk tuks on two wheels. I had become a bit nervous when a tuk tuk I was in took a corner fast, mainly because I didn't want to end up laid sideways in a tuk tuk. At the time it was a mixture of funny but quite scary. It was scary because we had been in a number of tuk tuks drivers that didn't really understand how roads, cars and the overturning of a tuk tuk worked, either that or they did and just didn't care. The funny part was watching five grown Indian men trying to pull this tuk tuk back onto four wheels, and two poor tourists stood there having completely no idea what was going on. They were completely fine, and no harm came to either of them, they just looked quite shocked, so since then we had been a little careful.

Anyway we made it back to the hostel safely, all in one piece and no overturned tuk tuk. We both grabbed a shower so we felt clean and fresh before our train ride, grabbed our backpacks and got in another tuk tuk to the train station.

I loved those train rides in India, it was kind of a break from all the hustle and bustle of India's city streets. I could just sit in my seat, with my headphones on, eat some tikka masala flavoured crisps, and watch everything out the window pass by. It was just so peaceful from inside the train, just going past the Indian countryside and small villages of people. The train ride was around four hours to Agra. The time passed quickly, they brought us food and hot tea again, we spoke about the Taj Mahal and what we both thought it might be like. It was a nice peaceful little 4 hour break from the hustle.

Around four hours later the train pulled into Agra station. We were both super excited to get to Agra. We had booked a homestay and it looked a bit nicer than a hostel, had a swimming pool or so we thought, but more about that later, and we were just both looking forward to a day of relaxing after getting up early to see the Taj. The train pulled in and to be honest Agra didn't look like anything special from the window of the train, although I'm not sure what I was expecting. We grabbed our backpacks as the train pulled in, jumped of the train, and as usual were bombarded by tuk tuk, taxi and donkey riders. Again we continued walking until we got out of the station and could gather our bearings, headed over to where a load of tuk tuks were parked and asked them if they could take us to our homestay, I cant remember exactly what it was called. We negotiated a price, and off we went. I already had a good idea of the prices we should be paying for tuk tuks as I knew the distances we were going in Delhi and how much it cost, so I just went with that, and knew when they were trying to rip us off.

The tuk tuk drivers in India always seemed to say they knew where you wanted to go, even if they didn't, they would say yes. They would then figure it out later, which was a bit annoying, as you would tell them exactly where, show them a google maps screenshot and they would nod saying 'yes yes come I know'. But really they had no clue. You would end up riding around some Indian city for 30 minutes while they ask random people on the street if they knew where it was, and would make me get my phone out to show them the map numerous times to these different people.

We had to book our train tickets to get to Rishikesh for the next day but unfortunately there were no train seats available for something ridiculous like the next two months. The tuk tuk driver that we found agreed to take us to a place where we could book buses. This would be our first Indian bus experience and by the end of it the worst bus experience of my life, but more on that later. He dropped us at a little bus booking office, and we went in. I asked the man behind the counter, saying that I needed a sleeper bus to Rishikesh for the day after today, he had a look at his schedule and said no buses. Me and Grandma gave each other that look, because we really didn't want to stay any longer than we had to in Agra, because there really wasn't much more to do, other than see the Taj Mahal. He then said in a broken English ' we have bus tomorrow, 11pm, sleeper'. I thought well that will have to do then, it's either that or stay in Agra till god knows when. We had booked two nights accommodation, but just thought we would have to deal with that later when we got there. It was a little over priced but we didn't have much choice.

The bus also had no air conditioning, but unfortunately it was the only bus. We were only supposed to be on it for 7 hours, from 11pm until 6am so we thought it wouldn't even be that hot anyway. Turns out we were on it for 17 hours, but again, more on that later. We got our tickets, organised a collection point, I also took his number, business name and address just in case the tickets were dodgy, not sure how much it would've helped in that situation, but better than nothing.

After a bit of searching for the homestay and shooting down a few back roads, we arrived. It looked quite nice from the outside, it was all fenced off. There was something really nice about pulling up here. It was set a little outside the main city of Agra. The property itself was fenced off and there was nothing either side of it, just some unfinished buildings dotted around that were set back from the road. As we pulled up there were a group of around 15 children just playing cricket in one of the open spaces next to the homestay, and the bright orange sun was setting in the horizon, reflecting of the half built buildings. It was really beautiful.

As we rang the doorbell to the homestay neither of us really knew what to expect, we had no idea what it would be like inside, what the guy would be like who's home it was, or if it would look anything like the photos. I mean it's always going to look better on booking.com than it actually is in person, especially when it was one of the cheapest places with a swimming pool you could find.

As the door opened a small Indian man greeted us, welcomed us in, and offered us some tea. He introduced himself, asked us about our journey, and we just had a friendly chat. He then asked if we had eaten and if we were hungry, we said yes, which we were. We were both starving as we hadn't eaten since on the train, and by the time we had settled in and had a chat with the guy it was about 7pm. He offered us a meal that had been cooked by his mother, we agreed and he went away to the kitchen to heat it all up. He came back and he had chapatis, different curries and some lentil dishes. It was incredible, the only thing was... he had no cutlery, so we had to get him to teach us how to make the chapati bread into a spoon to be able to eat it. My Grandma got the hang of it pretty quickly and was scooping it up like a pro. Whereas I had curry all over my fingers and face and bits of broken chapati bread in front of me. I just really couldn't get the hang of it. All in all, despite my experience with the chapati spoon making, the food was amazing. After eating we headed to our room for an early night as we had to be up at 3am the next day, ensuring we had enough time to get to the Taj Mahal for sunrise.

There were two time slots that you could go and see the Taj Mahal. Either at 4am in the morning for sunrise, or at 2pm in the afternoon. We had heard from a lot of people we had met travelling, and also from a few blogs online, that you had to go during sunrise. Even though it was an early wake up, it was a must. We thought seen as we were most likely only going to be here once, why not make the most of it and get up and see it at sunrise, especially as we had heard how beautiful it was. It was supposed to be the best time to see it, because as the sun rises it reflects off the white marble it is made from, creating a beautiful glistening effect. We could then just chill the rest of the day in the homestay where the pool was, play some cards and have a few drinks. Just relax and chill out before our 11pm overnight bus to Rishikesh.

Our last visit in Jaipur was to a place called the Amber Fort. Again, this did what it says on the tine, it was a fort and it was amber-coloured. It stood up on a hill, and when we got out of our tuk-tuk at the entrance one of the guys there was most concerned about me walking all that way uphill in the heat. He was very insistent that I should ride up in his car, of course.

However, I was having none of it! "I'm not that old and decrepit" says I! In fact it was a reasonably easy walk up, much less strenuous than the treks I did on a recent zip-wiring weekend I spent with the family!

We couldn't go inside the buildings as they were unsafe, but the architecture made it a fascinating place. The turrets, arches, courtyards and occasional stray goat made it a very interesting afternoon. So did the Indian visitors, who all seemed to want photos with one, the other, or both of us. If we had charged 10 rupee's (about 10p) per picture, I think we would have covered all of our holiday spending money, as "one picture, please" turned into one picture with each member of the family, some of which were quite large! Being set so high meant the views from the Fort were quite spectacular, taking in the lake at the foot of the hill, surrounding hills and a village nesting in the valley. All in all, a most enjoyable afternoon.

On our way back to the hostel, after being dropped off, a sandstorm blew up and we had to battle against the wind and stinging sand. Jake found it exciting as he had never been in a sandstorm before, but I was glad that I had my wrap-around sunglasses with me to keep the sand out of my eyes.

After another amazingly comfortable train ride we arrived in Agra. At last I was going to see the famous Taj Mahal. First we went to the booking office to book seats on a train to our next destination, only to find that the next available seats were on the day before we were due to come home. Such is the success of the Indian Railway! Of course, it being the pilgrimage time and us wanting to go to the holy place of Haridwar could have something to do with it.

Leaving the booking office we tried to get a tuk-tuk. This proved easier said than done. Perhaps because Agra is such an iconic place, all the tuk-tuk drivers wanted at least three times more than we were used to paying, so we declined them all. Eventually we managed to hire a taxi at a reasonable price to take us to the central bus station to book a ticket to Haridwar and then onto our accommodation. He, however, had a 'better' idea! He took us to a private bus company office, presumably owned by a friend. What a disaster!

If you ever go to India, avoid these companies like the plague. But, more of that later.

We were offered a place on an overnight sleeper for the following night. The price was way too high, but as we had to be at our next destination the day after we had little choice. Also, the bus had no air-conditioning, but as we were leaving at midnight and arriving at about six or seven in the morning, we thought that we would cope, so a deal was struck and we paid up.

We were then taken to our accommodation, which was no easy task, as it was about 10 minutes walk out of town and a bit tricky to find. By way of a change we had booked a home-stay for two nights. This means that we paid to stay in a private house with a family. We shared a twin room with a large en-suite shower room and the thing we were really looking forward to was a dip in the pool that was mentioned in the write-up.

After we had been shown to our room we asked the owner about the pool as we had seen no sign of one in what was little more than a yard outside. Our dreams of cool water and sun-loungers were fast disappearing, and they vanished completely as the owner, a little disconcerted, said it was on the roof, and that he had to fill it first. Two or three hours later the 'pool' was ready. I say 'pool' advisedly. It was a large rectangular concrete tank about 7 feet by 5 feet and 3-4 feet deep, with a built in concrete ledge about 18 inches below the waterline all the way around for sitting on. However, it looked cool, so Jake and I changed into our swimwear and climbed in. It was our turn to be disconcerted when the owner joined us! Apparently, living with the family meant just that, with the family joining in. However, we were able to have a few games of poker-dice on a tray provided by our host while sitting in the cool-ish water. Intense solar heat warmed the water up fairly quickly. The dice didn't always stay on the tray, but we usually managed to catch any that fell as they dropped through the water. Our host was fascinated by this activity and asked if he could take some photos for internet advertising, but I don't know if they ever appeared.

That evening our meal was an authentic Indian feast cooked by our hosts mother and brought from her house by his brother. They both joined us to eat a really delicious meal. Conversation was difficult here as our hosts' English was limited and quite heavily accented, but the whole stay was a unique experience and one I shall always remember.

Chapter 10 – Day 2 Agra

As hard as we thought it was going to be to wake up at 3am the following day, it was actually surprisingly easy. I think this was partly due to the fact that we were seeing the Taj Mahal that day, we were both super excited. We got up and off we set, we had ordered a tuk tuk to pick us up and take us to the main site for 3.15 as it took around 30 minutes to get there from where we were staying, and then it was a bit of a walk to the main gate.

About 30 minutes later we arrived at the entrance to the Taj Mahal. We were both very excited, as this was one of our main reasons for visiting India. We paid the tuk tuk driver and there was a big ticket office building. We went in and proceed to the tourist queue. In India, or most the places I visited they had a tourist queue and prices, and an Indian citizen queue and prices. We queued for about 10 minutes, paid and collected our tickets. They also gave us a bottle of water and these shoe covers. These were just thin shoe shape style socks that you had to put over your shoes. They were clean and I guess helped prevent scuffing on the floor of the Taj Mahal, so everyone had to wear them.

After collecting all these bits and pieces we were lead out to a bus, we could either take the bus which was about 10 minutes, or walk which was about 25 minutes, which would then take us right up to the entrance gates of the Taj Mahal. We decided to walk, as the queue for the bus was pretty long, and we thought it might help wake us up a little bit.

As we walked towards the entrance, we spoke about how awesome it was to finally be here, actually seeing the Taj Mahal. We laughed at the fact who would've thought 5 weeks ago that me and Grandma would be walking up to the Taj Mahal together, certainly not me, and I'm even more certain she wouldn't have believed it.

At the entrance to the grounds of the Taj Mahal, we had our tickets checked and then we entered. We still couldn't see it, we walked for about 5 more minutes and then it just appeared. As cliché as it sounds it really was quite magical, and I think it was made even more incredible by the fact I was sharing this experience with my Grandma. The sun was rising over the top of the Taj, which gave it this incredible glistening effect, like something out of a film. It really was incredible, and still to this day is one of the most incredible sights I have ever seen. We both just stood and admired its beauty for a good 10 minutes. It wasn't long until I had my phone out and was taking pictures, and my Grandma had her camera out…. I don't think her phone could take photos. It really was beautiful, we took a few photos of ourselves, and then went for a walk around.

We spent a good hour walking around, looking at it from all different angles, and even went inside, it truly was incredible. Built into the white marble walls of the tomb are bright precious stones of ruby, jade, gold and other precious stones and metals. It really is quite incredible considering the Taj Mahal was built in around 1653. It's quite amazing how something so beautiful and complex was built so many years ago, and it really does take your breath away.

We continued to walk around it and take in the beauty of the tomb, and then we wandered into the gardens surrounding it. We found a little marble bench from where we could see the Taj, and just sat down. We people watched and took in where we were. We must have been sat there for about an hour and a half, until we decided it was time to leave. We literally had to drag ourselves away. It was strange thinking I will probably never see this again, it was a strange feeling. I think it was just the feeling from finally being there and seeing it, and then leaving, the time passed so quickly. It was now about 6.30am and we were both getting pretty hungry, we headed out of the entrance, walked back and got a tuk tuk back to near the homestay, not before a stop for breakfast though.

I had noticed on our way to the Taj Mahal that there was a subway, not far from our homestay, and I know they do breakfast style subs. We decided to get a subway as it we had now been up for 4 hours and were both getting ready for breakfast. We got dropped of at subway, and god damn was it good. I went for a foot long sub of course, my Grandma just a 6 inch and we both had a coffee too. We finished up our subs, and headed to the supermarket to grab some snacks and juice for the rest of the day.

We decided we would just spend the rest of the day chilling out, as we had a bus to catch that evening. We got back, went into the room and just chilled out on the bed. It wasn't long before my Grandma fell asleep, finally I could get her back for teasing me about falling asleep in one of the temples we visited in New Delhi.

She woke up not long after and we thought we would take a dip in the pool again and just chill out for a bit before our bus later that evening. The bus wasn't until 11pm so we didn't have to leave the homestay until about 10pm, 9.30 just to be safe. Ginesh I think his name was, the guy that owned and ran the homestay, I'm pretty sure it was Ginesh. For the book, that's what we'll go by anyway. Ginesh put the pool on for us, in the photos on booking.com it looked like a pool but it was more of a dunk tank, only being about 3 meters by 3 meters wide. It was good enough for us though. We both just chilled out in the pool, played some games and relaxed. We each did some reading, played some cards, and we packed our bags and got ready for our bus later that evening. It was really nice to just chill out and not do a lot for the afternoon. It was good to just relax and not have to go anywhere.

We had one last meal provided by Ginesh's mother and then we grabbed our backpacks, hopped in the tuk tuk that we had pre-arranged earlier that day, and of he took us to the bus station, not of course without having to find directions to it from people in the street. Even though he said he knew where it was. (That's one of my top tips if you're planning on travelling to India, always leave thirty minutes earlier than you think you need. Just to allow whoever it is driving you time to find your destination). I thought the next part of our India adventure needed its own chapter, as it's one of our most stand out memories of India, and not necessarily for good reasons. Although we look back at it now and laugh, it was definitely a character building moment.

The next morning we were up before dawn as the Taj Mahal is best seen at sunrise. I could barely contain my excitement. I was about to fulfil a lifetimes ambition and visit one of the last must-see places on my list!

After agreeing a return journey price, we were off. On arrival at our destination we paid our entrance fee and were given some shoe covers as it was too large and busy a site to ask visitors to remove their shoes. These covers came in one size only and didn't cater for anyone with a shoe size much above a six. Mine were not too bad, but Jake's very quickly disintegrated so he eventually gave up on them. Looking around us we found that he was not the only one!

With a deep breath we then left the imposing building that con situated the entrance and had our first sight of a distant Taj Mahal! For me, it didn't disappoint, even with three of the turrets surrounded by heavy mesh for maintenance work. It seemed to have a glow about it, even in the half-lighted. It was a slightly overcast morning so we were treated to an impressive monochrome scene. As the sun slowly rose, seen from the mausoleum was a dark silhouette against a pearly grey sky, while viewed from the other side the sun's rays gave the carved white marble a golden shine. An eager Indian took us to the Mosque situated across the plaza to one side. Here, one of the archways formed a perfect frame for the Taj Mahal with the now risen sun shining like a spotlight just about to break free from behind it. As the sun rose higher the hazy cloud was burned off and the mausoleum was revealed in all it's dazzling beauty, gleaming white against an azure sky.

We spent a couple of hours walking round the building and the site, exploring the tree-shaped paths. We took many photos, but the ubiquitous 'professional' photographer was present, keen to take photos of us both for a small fee of course. In fact, he used our cameras so we didn't have to buy the photos and it turned out to be a reasonable way to get some unusual shots, including, of course, the famous 'Diane seat'. We were taken inside by another eager Indian keen to show us the treasures there. The mausoleum contains two tombs, a small one for the Rajah and a much larger one for his beloved wife. The walls consist of beautifully carved panels inlaid with gold and precious gems which glow translucent red and green when light is shone on them. Again, no photos were allowed by it is a memory that will live with me forever. Jake and I were surprised how un-crowded it was. There were few Europeans and not that many Indians visiting. We came to the conclusion that it must be because the height of summer is considered to be the quite season because of the extreme heat.

Finally, tearing ourselves away we said goodbye to the Taj Mahal and went to find our driver. Not long into the journey home Jake was offered the chance to drive. Naturally, he jumped at it and so began his lesson on the Indian highway code. This consists mainly of putting ones hand on the horn and driving full tilt into impossible small gaps in the traffic. All in all, he did a very good job. By the time we got back to our digs he was squeezing through those gaps with an inch to spare as if he had been doing it all his life!

On returning to our room I propped myself on my bed with my book and promptly fell asleep. After all, I had been up since silly o'clock and it was now afternoon, so it was my turn for a daytime nap. (Jake had his in the shade at the Red Fort on our very first day.) This was followed by more poker-dice in the 'pool' with our host, a shower and another delicious meal cooked by his mother.

As we were leaving before midnight instead of staying the full night as originally planned, Jake negotiated a slight reduction in our charges and we parted company with our host with expressions of good-will all round.

Chapter 11– The Bus Journey From Hell, Agra to Rishikesh

So it was time to get our bus from Agra to Rishikesh, we arrived at the supposed stop around 10:30pm, the bus was due to leave at 11pm, so we had some time to spare. The bus finally arrived at about 11.30pm, we had been waiting for an hour by the side of the road. It wasn't an actual bus stop as such that we were getting picked up from, it was just down the side of some road, outside a shop. There was another couple waiting with us who were heading up to Rishikesh, so we knew we were in the right place.

The bus had a very strange layout, it had flat beds at the top which fit two people, it was basically a thin mattress about 3 inches thick on some metal beams. Then underneath this were seats which laid down into beds, but it wasn't really seats, more just cushions on metal beams. It wasn't comfortable at all. It was also pretty hot on the bus, so I cracked open the window to allow some air to blow in while we tried to get some sleep. I just remember thinking this is okay, I can deal with this. The bus left at 11.30pm which means we should be arriving into Rishikesh at around 6.30am. Just before the weather starts heating up, and hopefully we can both sleep a few hours of the journey, so it wouldn't seem that long.

I put my ear plugs in and my eye mask on, and used my rucksack as a pillow My Grandma put her eye mask on and we both tried to get some sleep.

About 7 hours later we both took our eye masks of and sat up, both having been in and out of sleep the whole night. It was kind of hard to get into a deep sleep when all four wheels on the bus kept leaving the ground, and every car, bus or cow we passed seemed to make a noise for no apparent reason, but we made do with it, and made the best out of the situation.

It came to about 6.30 and we both decided we might as well get up and down from the bunks as we would be arriving in under an hour. We both sat up, rubbed our eyes and hopped down from the beds that were at the top of the bus. Many people were already sat up, and all of the bottom beds had already been converted into seats. So we sat down in two of the seats and just waited for the bus to arrive.

It came to about 8.30am and it was starting to heat up, we were now about 2 hours late past our arrival time, and I was getting a little impatient as we were due to arrive so long ago. I gave it another hour or so, and the bus started to slow down, we were almost not moving at this point and it seemed we were stuck in some serious traffic. It got to the point that we were moving that slow that people were getting on and off the bus to use the toilet, and to go to the shops/stalls to get food and water.

It was now about 10am... 3.5 hours late. So I just decided to start asking people what was going on, as I was getting super impatient and kind of wanted to be in the know. I asked around a few people didn't understand me, and then one guy began talking to us. An Indian guy but he spoke very good English. He went on to explain that there is a festival in the local town next to Rishikesh, called Haridwar. This is why there is all the traffic, because everyone is going to this holy festival on some sort of pilgrimage.

I grabbed my phone out my backpack to check on google maps exactly where we were, and how far out we were. Only to realise that we were just over half way there. I looked at my Grandma showed her the map and said 'what a bloody day to pick to travel to Rishikesh, there's only a holy festival going on at the neighbouring town'. She was actually really chilled about it, and just sat there with a smile, that was until we hit a bump in the road and she smacked her head on the top of the bus. I panicked a little bit and rushed over to make sure she was okay. I think it was more the shock, she just laid down for a little while and was soon up and sat there smiling again, I think she was just loving the adventure.

I jumped of the bus and went to the toilet, also grabbed some crisps, a couple of mango juices and some water. We were all out of water, and we were both pretty in need of a drink and something to eat. A few more hours past and we were still crawling along in this traffic, the bus was literally going at walking speed. We both just tried to make the best of it, we were talking to the locals on the bus, chatting among ourselves and also tried to get more sleep. We just tried to make the best out of a bad situation and kept ourselves busy.

It was really starting to heat up now, as it

approached midday and 40c. But luckily the bus was moving faster now, so the breeze was quite nice coming in from the window, it helped to ventilate and cool the bus down a bit. We continued driving for about 3 more hours and we finally arrived at Haridwar, nope not Rishikesh. Still not our stop, but Haridwar, the small town before ours where the holy festival was. We were then told by the driver that this was where the bus stopped as it couldn't go any further due to the festival. We both though oh great, just what we need after sitting on a bus with no air con for 16 hours in the middle of the Indian summer.

Once we were of the bus and had collected our backpacks from underneath its rickety frame, we spoke to the couple we had met while waiting for the bus in Agra. They were also heading to Rishikesh, so we decided to split a tuk tuk fare into the city. We all climbed into a tuk tuk and got a price to Rishikesh that seemed reasonable. There weren't many free tuk tuk's around so we were pretty lucky to get one, especially so quickly. It was absolutely crazy, everywhere was busy, there were cars and people piled into tuk tuks and on motorbikes. I had never seen anything like it. About three more people got into our tuk tuk for a ride, god knows how they all managed to fit in, especially with our backpacks in there. I swear there was someone stood on the back too. There was no less than 7 people to a tuk tuk. The roads were jammed, and everyone was looking for a ride.

I was so tired and hungry, I really wasn't paying much attention, about another 30 minutes later we arrived at the bottom of Rishikesh, the locals got off and left rather quickly.

We still weren't at our hostel, which he agreed to take us to, as I showed him the address on my phone before we left. The couple gave us their share of the money, said goodbye and headed off. We stayed in the tuk tuk and he looked at us expecting us to get out. I said no we need to go to the hostel, and showed him on the map again, he understood, drove a little further and said it's up there, you can walk. I was like okay, but I didn't believe this guy, he just wanted us out. I told my Grandma to wait in the tuk tuk while I had a little walk up to see what was up there…

Nothing, no hostel to be seen. I walked back and said no it's not up there and got it up on google maps with my screenshot, he literally had no idea.

He then started to kick off, so we argued back that he hadn't taken us to our hostel yet, and he argued back saying he can't take us any further. Enough was enough, so we then shouted over two police officers who were stood a little further up. They spoke to the driver, we showed them the map and the police officers must have told him in which direction to go as he soon headed off.

It was about 20 minutes later and up the hillside into the Himalayan mountains, and he was asking more people where the hostel was. He really had no idea, again even though he said he knew where it was when we got in the taxi.

About 45 minutes later and the asking about 10 different people, Grandma spotted the Zostel sign in the corner of her eye. We pulled up outside the hostel, paid the tuk tuk driver and walked into the hostel.

Finally we had made it.

I looked at my phone and it said 4.30pm. It wasn't the 8 hour journey we thought it was going to be. 17 and a half hours later, we had finally made it to the hostel.

We both entered and decided to get and early night. This hostel seemed much more friendly than the other ones we had stayed in, it seemed much more sociable and had beautiful views over the vibrant green mountains.

We went into the hostel, checked in, dropped our bags and grabbed what was one of the best showers of my life. W then went and had some food at a local place down the road. It was amazing to finally have a hot cooked meal, something other than crisps, which is all we had eaten for the past 18 hours. We then headed back to the hostel, chilled on the rooftop for about an hour and headed to bed. We were both shattered and thought we deserved a good nights sleep.

We made our way to the bus company's office, if you could call it that, in plenty of time for our midnight bus. There we met a couple who has been told ten o'clock. They were still waiting!

About an hour later, after pressing the 'clerk' for information, we were told that our bus had been cancelled. However, there were seats available on a non-sleeper bus arriving 'soon'! I immediately demanded a large proportion of our money back. Strangely enough, within five minutes a sleeper bus appeared across the road with space for all four of us!

The one thing I will never understand is why Jake and I were given a top bunk while the young couple were given two single ones across the aisle.

Without waiting for me to reach the bunk and with a jerk that nearly knocked me off the ladder, we were off. That start should have warned us of what was to come! The bus sounded as if every nut and bolt was loose, it rattled so much and it seemed to hit every pothole in the road at top speed. I was on the outside of the bunk and slept very fitfully as I was afraid of being bounced out.

Morning came eventually and the bottom bunks were converted back to seats, but things got no better. Arrival time of six o'clock came and went, the bus got hotter and hotter and Haridwar seemed no closer. Vendors along the road did a roaring trade of cold bottled water and mango juice, exchanging goods and money through the windows. The Indian passengers obviously knew what to expect as they all seemed to have brought food, but expecting to reach our destination in time for breakfast we had not. All we had were some crisps and biscuits in our small bags. As I recall we had one 'comfort' stop where we managed to grab a snack and some more water. I almost felt like a poor cow we saw, foraging in a rubbish cart.

The worst moment was sitting looking out of the window and the bus hit what felt like a crater at top speed, I was bounced so high off the seat that I cracked my head hard on the underside of the bunk above. I saw stars. Jake was sitting across the aisle a little further down the bus, but one of the other passengers called him back. They were all very kind, remade the bunk and urged me to lie down. However, when I did I just felt sick, partly because of the bouncing of the bus, so the bunk was converted back to seats. Jake looked after me very well, refusing to return to his former seat, even after I felt that I had recovered. He spent the rest of the journey in a small seat at the end of the aisle at the back of the bus! At the time this seemed like the journey from hell, but time mellows the memory, although Jake says that it was the worst bus journey he has ever taken. At last we arrived in Haridwar at about two p.m. Both the young couple, from Agra, and us were going to Rishikesh so we agreed to share a tuk-tuk. There began a new adventure!

The seats in a tuk-tuk will just about take three, forward and rearward facing, and the luggage storage at the back is very small. After striking a deal to drop us off in turn, we crammed one backpack behind the seat, as this filled the storage space, the other three were piled into the tuk-tuk with the four of us. Imagine our surprise when the driver stopped to pick up an Indian family of three! He insisted that we were to move our luggage to the rear space. We refused, as it would simply have fallen off the back, and indicating in our turn that they had to share the front seat with him as we were paying him a good price for the hire of his vehicle. After a few minutes the young boy was able to sit on a small space at the side of the rear-facing seats, but as there was a backpack on the floor his feet were sticking out of the side. Given the Indian habits of driving to within an inch of the other vehicles we didn't feel this was safe, so we squeezed a gap for him to put his feet. I must say that never on any other occasion were we expected to share our tuk-tuk!

After dropping off our extra passengers we finally arrived on the main street of Rishikesh, where our driver assured us we were all within a few minutes walk of our destinations. The young couple gave us their share of the money and got out, but Jake and I had had an experience of 'not far' and 'a few minutes walk' in Delhi so we refused, saying we wanted to be taken to the hostel. The driver asked to be paid and we said "when we arrive". Jake had shown him the name and address of the hostel, but he still seemed very confused. The fact that his English was very limited didn't help. He appeared hopelessly lost, even after asking for directions several times. We ended up on the other side of Rishikesh, after passing, picking up and re-dropping off the young couple on the way. He was now adamant that we should get out, but we were equally adamant we wouldn't until we arrived out our desired destination.

Eventually he drove back into Rishikesh and called over a passing policeman. Luckily he spoke English and after an excited conversation with our driver we learnt the cause of his agitation. Hew thought that the young couple had left without paying and that we were refusing to pay. We explained that we had all of the money and that he would be paid in full when we reached our destination but not before. At this point he calmed down a little. Jake showed the policeman the paper with the name and address of the hostel and after another conversation with the driver, we set off...again!

This time we spotted the sign for our hostel, much higher up than we expected which is why we missed it in the first place. After paying a relieved driver, who was glad to see the back of us I think, we finally checked in over an hour and a half after our arrival into Rishikesh.

At last, after nearly sixteen hours of a nightmare journey we had reached the hoped for tranquillity of the yoga capital of the world.

Chapter 12– Day 1 Rishikesh

Today we didn't set a time to meet, we thought we needed a lie in considering our bus journey last night. It felt so amazing getting into a normal bed that evening, no bumping up and down, no car horns... and a pillow. I slept like a baby, waking up at about 9.30am. By the time I had given myself time to wake up, grabbed a shower and got dressed it was about 10.30am.

I headed up to the roof which is where me and my Grandma arranged to meet the in the morning. The hostel we were staying in called Zostel had this amazing rooftop that overlooked the Himalayas, as you looked around it was just this lush green mountainous landscape. It was really beautiful. My Grandma was already up, which I kind of knew she would be, she was just sat on the rooftop reading her book. We decided to grab breakfast in the hostel and chill for a little bit before heading out and exploring Rishikesh for the first time.

We had four days in total in Rishikesh, 5 nights. So we had plenty of time to explore. Rishikesh was my favourite of all the places I visited in India. It was so peaceful and just naturally beautiful, much more so than the cities we had visited so far. After our breakfast which consisted of naan bread and coffee, we decided to head out and see what there was to do in the city. We had a wander down the road and there were loads of local excursion shops, they were all selling different activities, we thought we would have a look and see what they had to do.

We went into a few of these shops until we found one that was willing to give us a good price, and then we had a look at the activities we wanted to do. I wanted to do a yoga class, since were in the yoga capital of the world, Grandma was happy to do this, so we decided to do this one day. We also both quite liked the idea of white water rafting down the river Ganges. We decided to get that booked for the following morning too. It was something my Grandma had always wanted to try, something she wanted to tick of her bucket list, so it was pretty awesome she got to do it on the Ganges of India. Even more so when it only cost us about £5 each for the whole morning. Grandma was also quite interested in zip lining, but it was pretty expensive so we decided against it, and thought we would save it for another day.

After booking our trips, we decided to go for a walk across the famous suspension bridge called Lakshman Jhula. The bridge connects two small villages in Rishikesh. There is then another bridge further down the river. So our plan was to cross Lakshman Jhula, walk down the other side of the river through the mountain path, then cross over the other bridge and walk back up the other side to our hostel. We began walking to Lakshman Jhula down this windy little road that led us to the bridge, and we stumbled across the cool little second hand book store and coffee shop. It overlooked the Ganges and lower mountains so we decided to stop, look at some of the books, and grab a coffee. I really fancied one of the fresh juices, but they often mix it with water, and it's just not worth the stomach ache after, so I decided on coffee in the end. We sat and drank our coffees and looked out over the Ganges. It was beautiful, just sat in this little cafe surrounded by such a beautiful landscape. We both just took it all in and people watched below. After about 20 minutes we had both finished our coffees. We had a little look around the book shop, and then decided to carry on our walk across the bridge.

We walked down the little steps that led up to the cafe, turned the corner and began to walk across Lakshman Jhula. The bridge though was not just for pedestrians, it was also shared with motorcycles, dogs and even cows. You would be quite happily walking across the bridge, grabbing some photos and then get this big cow coming straight at you and have to move to the side. This wouldn't have been a problem but the bridge was only about 4ft wide, and when the cow is 2ft wide, it doesn't leave much room. We wandered across the bridge and took some pictures along the way, the views from either side were amazing, and the you could see the water rushing right down 70ft beneath the bridge. After about 10 minutes of walking we made it to the other side, where we had a look around, took some more pictures and stopped for a mouthful of water.

We continued to walk down the other side of the Ganges, along the dirt road, either side high with trees. You couldn't really see the river now, it was quite dense with trees either side of the dirt road. There seemed to be many people walking along this road, I guess it was a busy route. We continued further down until we got near to the bottom of the river, close to where the other bridge was. There was so much life to the city, there were locals cooking from big pots that were sitting on top of open wood fires. People selling things, and just the hustle and bustle in general was quite fascinating to watch. We continued over to the other side of the bridge where the bridge almost met with the water. There were many local people down by the river, washing themselves, washing their clothes and children playing, the water towards the bottom end of the city was pretty strong, but it didn't stop the children playing in it.

We just sat and watched for a good hour, it felt so peaceful, even though there was plenty to be heard, it still felt peaceful down the bottom of the river. There was so much going on, I could've sat there and people watched for hours. We decided it was probably time to get up and continue walking back up the hill towards to hostel as it was around 3pm by the time we had finished people watching. We walked for another 20 minutes and came across a bunch of young people playing cricket right by the banks of the Ganges. We thought it seemed another perfect place to do some more people watching. The scenery around really was such a contrast compared to the cities we had visited before. High green mountains all around with the river Ganges running right through the middle, then the mixture of shanty built houses, temples and brick buildings situated all around the mountain side and the bright blue sky. It really made for a beautiful setting.

After about another hour we continued our walk up the mountainside up towards the hostel. It was hard finding the right way to go. I was trying my best through using google maps on my phone, but no matter where it seemed to take me, we seemed to end up in some random area which just consisted of the local residents houses. It took us around another hour until we found the main road. We decided to just follow this back up to the top as this was probably the safest option and would save us getting lost. We followed the busy road all the way back up to the top, it took us about an hour more to walk all the way back to the hostel. I don't think we quite realised how far we had actually walked. We stopped along the way to take more pictures of the scenery before finally making it back up to the hostel. We both grabbed showers and then went to sit on the rooftop of the hostel while we decided where we were going to eat that evening.

This hostel was by far the most sociable hostel we had stayed in while being in India, it was actually busy, the previous few hostels we stayed in didn't have much life to them, so it was a nice change. We sat down, had a drink and ended up meeting a few other people. It was such a nice change to actually have a few other people in the hostels. I think further down south they didn't have many people as it was low season and too hot. After a little while a few of the group we had got talking to decided they were going to eat at this restaurant called the little Buddha.

After everyone was ready, we all headed of to the restaurant which was about 15 minute walk away, back across the bridge. One of the guys we were with had been before, so he was leading the way, and about 15 minutes later we arrived. We walked up this thin set of stairs into the restaurant. It was so beautiful, it was the cool little cafe up in the hills on the banks of the Ganges, the views from the top were incredible. You could see right out into the mountains, and all along the bank of the river. We sat down and ordered some food, which I must say was incredible. I think in total we ate there 5-6 times during our stay in Rishikesh. I can't remember what Grandma ordered, but I had palak paneer and a garlic naan bread. It was definitely the best food I had eaten since being in India, it was incredible. All in all we had an enjoyable night. Amazing food, some incredible views, and there were finally some cool people to chill out with from the hostel. After a little while we grabbed the bill, paid up and headed back to the hostel across the bridge. It was still pretty busy outside, plenty of people walking around and it was about 21.30 in the evening.

We got back to the hostel, and we all went and sat up on the rooftop, we continued talking and telling stories until about 11pm which was when most people went back to the rooms to get some sleep. We headed off too, since we had our 3 hour yoga class the next morning... Well what I thought was going to be yoga.

This was most definitely my most enjoyable day yet in India. I loved the city, the food, the people and the beautiful walk along the banks. I was already beginning to fall in love with Rishikesh.

After our previous hostels where everyone

seemed to keep to themselves, Zostel in Rishikesh was an eye-opener. Everyone was really friendly and we all gathered in one big group in the evenings.

Breakfast wasn't included here, but afternoon tea and snacks were provided on the roof. The hostel boasted a good restaurant, so we usually bought our breakfast and took it out to the roof to eat, but we were usually out and about for both lunch and dinner. In fact, we spent most of our evenings in Rishikesh all gathered together in a restaurant called the Little Buddha. This was a semi-open-air restaurant boasting a large balcony that extended out over the Ganges. Amazing food, amazing panoramic views and excellent company, what more could anyone ask for!?

According to legend the town is build on the site where two brothers were wanting to cross to do penance on the other side. One braved the raging torrent to carry a rope across so the other could make the crossing. There is now a narrow bridge at the side. Although only about four feet wide, this bridge is always crammed with traffic. It carried not only pedestrians, but also bicycles, scooters, motorbikes and even the *occasional cow! The main hazard, however, were the monkeys. They lined the uprights and the suspension cables just waiting for their chance to leap upon an unwary traveller. Children kept their snacks and ice-creams very close to their bodies, while I usually took my precious Tilly hat off until I had reached the other side. At one end of the bridge were shops and cafes, while at the other end was a beautiful Sikh Pagoda. It was possible to go in but being near the start of the monsoon season, we had some rain and the ground seemed permanently muddy, probably because of all of the footfall. As we had to take our shoes off as usual, we decided that we didn't want to walk around with muddy feet all day. We were going to walk along the river, and it would have been most uncomfortable.*

As mentioned previously, we arrived at the festival of pilgrimage. The Ganges, or Ganga, as it is known locally, is considered a holy river and the banks were crowded as far as the eye could see with people bathing in its water to purify themselves. Every possible access point was a mass of colour as most of the women wore colourful sari's and the men wearing the traditional white trousers and tunic.

Interspersed with these were others in European dress, so it was a very cosmopolitan scene. As I said earlier, Rishikesh is the yoga capital of the world, being where the Beatles met with Maharishi, and as a result it doesn't seem to have the frantic feel of the other Indian cities. Life seems to flow at a much more leisurely pace.

Chapter 13 – Day 2 Rishikesh

Today we woke up pretty early, at about 8am as we had to be outside the excursion office for 11am, we grabbed showers, and by the time we were ready it was about 9am. We then went upstairs on the rooftop and decided to get some breakfast. Breakfast for us while we were in Rishikesh just usually consisted of some sort of naan bread. Neither of us really minded, as the naan bread in India was always amazing. They also had other options such as eggs cooked different ways on toast, omelettes, toast and jams. I sometimes had the eggs or sometimes just had a garlic naan for breakfast, I'm sure everyone I spoke to wished I hadn't with my garlic breath, but it tasted great, so I didn't really care. They also did the most amazing coffees in the hostel, it didn't taste the same as coffee back in England, it had a different taste to it. I don't really know how to explain it, but it was nice, particularly if you like strong coffee. After chilling out on the rooftop for about an hour and eating breakfast, we decided to head of to the excursion store where we were to meet the guy for our 3 hour yoga class. The class was due to start at 11am, but we were due to get there for 10.30am, 30 minutes early to give us time to find the yoga hall, wherever we were going. We really had no idea what to expect, who it was going to be teaching us, or where we would be having this yoga class.

We arrived at the excursion office after about a 10 minute walk down the hill, and the owner of the tour operator was there to meet us. He said the actual place where we would be doing the yoga was about 10 minutes away, and he offered us the back of a motorbike, my Grandma didn't want to do this, not out of fear, but due to other circumstances, so we decided to walk. It was about a 20 minute walk until we arrived. When we arrived at the entrance to this old looking building, a bearded man was stood outside. He had long brown hair and was wearing wearing long orange robes, I presume he was some sort of Buddhist monk.

He kindly greeted us with a gentle hand shake and bow of the head, me and my Grandma I guess out of courtesy and a natural reaction, reacted in the same way back to him, he seemed very mellow and relaxed. He asked our names, and then he asked us to follow him into this old building, we followed him down these empty corridors, which had various paintings hung in them, of whom I don't know, but I'm guessing were some sort of religious icon. After walking for a couple of minutes along these corridors we came to a large empty room. It was slightly dark, and didn't really have any windows, there were multiple different paintings around the room, and it had a hard laminate floor.

When we first got into the room, he asked us if we had done yoga/meditation before, we both explained our own personal experiences and then he gave us two roll out yoga mats, and said 'now we begin'.

We started of with just sitting there, hands on our knees and with our eyes closed. After about 10 minutes he started chanting some sort of mantra. After about 10 minutes he then asked us to join in, I mean I don't mind trying new stuff and it was fun, but I'm pretty sure we signed up for a yoga class, not a mantra class. Anyway, as he asked us to join in and follow his lead repeating after him, I slowly opened my right eye, as my Grandma was sat to the right of me. I noticed he (the teacher) has his eyes closed still, so I gave a quick look at my Grandma and she too was looking at me, we both just gave this huge smirk at each other to sort of say 'what on earth have we got ourselves into this time'. This sitting with our eyes close chanting must have continued for a good further 50 minutes. I lost track of time as there was no clock in the room and we put our mobiles over to the side before we began the class. After this he asked us to lay on our backs, he continued chanting and just asked us to lay there and think of nothing. I'm guessing it was more of a meditation than a yoga session, as the class literally consisted of no yoga whatsoever. We were laid there for a good hour while he continue to chant, occasionally he would walk over and press his thumb in the middle of our foreheads. The first time it made me jump as I was so zoned out, just laid on the floor. It was such strange feeling, I think because we had been laid there while he chanted away these mantras for so long we kind of got lost in it, it was quite a strange experience, but all in all a good one.

After a little while, he asked us to sit back up and then stand, then he concluded that the class was over. We thanked him and then he invited us to go get a drink just around the corner, we politely said yes and followed him around some gardens and under little arches throughout this stone wall built complex, until we came to a little stone like terrace. There were many other Buddhists/monks sat out on the stone terrace in their orange robes. He offered us a drink, again the same as in Delhi it was this pink water. We both took it in our hands but neither of us drank it, as we were sure it would've been made with tap water which would have given us some serious belly ache. I think we both just had a couple of sips out of pure politeness. He was still speaking to us, asking us how we found the class, and then he happened to mention that one of the monks, who was sat in front of us had not spoken for 17 years. '17 years' I repeated, I really couldn't believe it. But apparently it is quite popular for Buddhists to go on these vows of silence for incredibly long periods. Still though I thought, 17 years and not a word, I found it very impressive.

I asked him why and it was quite interesting, apparently it was because when we speak we use up so much energy, and by going very long periods without speaking, we contain all this energy within us, and it can be used for other things. It is said to help them on the path to enlightenment, I think that was the basic gist of it. I was still astonished for a few days after, and still am to this day that someone could possibly go that long without speaking.

After sitting there for 10 minutes or so we decided to leave and head back to the hostel, we said goodbye and then he pointed us in the direction of the entrance and the way out of the big stone complex. We found our way out and headed back up to the hostel. By the time we got to the hostel it was about 3.30pm. We decided we were just going to chill out for the afternoon, have a coffee in the hostel, read a little and maybe play some cards. After chilling out for a couple of hours, a few more people appeared on the roof terrace. We also re met with a few people whom we went to dinner with the night before, we all just chilled out and spoke for a little while again, and decided to head back to the little Buddha since the food was so good last time. We all left at about 6 and walked down the hill a little, crossed the same busy bridge that had people, scooters and cows wandering across it, and then headed up the little wooden stairway into the little Buddha.

The guys that owned the restaurant were Nepalese and they were really nice. We all sat down at a big wooden table in the middle of the room, and ordered a few drinks, as I mentioned before, you couldn't buy alcohol anywhere in Rishikesh, so there were no beers on the menu, it was all juices, tea's and fresh natural products. We usually just stuck to water as it was cheaper, then we ordered food. I ordered some momo, this was another one of my favourite dishes in India, they were amazing. These were like little dumplings filled with vegetables, and they came with some different dipping sauces, again they were amazing. I think they are more of a Nepalese style food, but are heavily influenced in India, and very popular, and oh my do they taste amazing. In the little Buddha the momo were the best, as they came with a little soy sauce pot, and when dipped in that they were so good.

It sounds just like a starter but it's enough, you get about 12 dumplings and this soup with it, I also got a garlic and cheese naan bread to go with it. Everyone else ordered their dishes, and we sat there talking and eating till about 9pm. Then we decided to head back to the hostel, me and Grandma had white water rafting the following day, it wasn't until the afternoon, but we were both still feeling pretty tired and decided to get a reasonably early night. By the time we walked back, got changed, and managed to switch of and fall asleep it must've been about 10.30pm.

Jake is very much into yoga, so he was keen to take part in a yoga session here. I agreed to do one with him as I'm always up for new experiences. Well, some new experiences, anyway! We duly booked the session and turned up where instructed on the day full of anticipation.

Eventually a guy turned up on a motorbike and invited us to jump on for the journey down the road to the yoga community where our yogi awaited us. I flatly refused, not through fear of traffic, but because of other circumstances. We were assured that our destination was only a short walk down the road so I told Jake to ride and I would go on foot. Understanding my reasons, Jake refused to let me walk alone, so off we set together. Amazingly, it was not Indian distance and we soon arrived at our destination. A tall, dignified man in a long robe was waiting for us.

After a greeting, we were ushered into a large hall, shoeless. Naturally supplied with mats and invited to sit down. We were expecting a couple of hours of yoga and meditation, but what we got was very different. We were asked to sit cross-legged on out mats, lotus position if possible. You must be joking! We then were asked to close our eyes, join our thumbs and forefingers together in a circle, and, resting our heads on our knees, empty our minds. There followed about an hour of meditation. I can't be exactly sure how long this part of the session lasted as, try as I might, I could not see my watch. All I know is that after five to ten minutes my mind, far from being empty, was full with thoughts of how uncomfortable I was. I struggle with sitting on the floor at the best of times, never mind cross-legged, so I got very fidgety. Unable to keep it straight for very long, my back also began to ache.

What a relief it was to be told to lie on our backs. I found this a far more comfortable position for meditation and was at last able to relax my mind. Every so often our yogi would place his fore and index fingers on our foreheads and press gently but firmly. This gave me a very strange sensation that I find hard to describe. It was an energizing buzz, but also very calming. I have never felt anything like it before or since. After a while we turned onto our tummies, then finished in the sitting position again. After our three hour session we were taken to the communal area, where we met more of the community residents, and were offered bananas and the sweet pink drink we had first tried in the Sikh Temple in Delhi. This time we politely refused as we had our own bottles of water.

All in all, it was not my best experience in India, and we were both disappointed that we got no actual yoga.

Chapter 14 – Day 3 Rishikesh

We woke up at about 8 and good job as I got a call from the white water rafting office saying that we needed to start the excursion at 10am. We were originally supposed to be going white water rafting at 1pm, but it's liable to change due to weather conditions and the rapids have to be safe and be suitable conditions to take tourists out on. I quickly found my Grandma and let her know that we would need to be leaving at 9.30, as we were now rafting at 10am. She had a little look of shock on her face, she was a little nervous about it, mainly because of her glasses, as she needed them to stay on her face so she could see, and was worried they would fall off. But she didn't let it stop her and still signed up, it was another thing she wanted to tick of her bucket list, so there was no stopping her.

We quickly got everything together, I covered myself in sunscreen and went to meet my Grandma. We walked down the road to the tour agency, and there was a white land rover already waiting outside, we double checked with the guide to make sure we had everything we needed and then squeezed in the back. We had to drive to the banks of the river where we would begin our trip down the rapids of the Ganges. I remember thinking to myself, this is awesome, a half day white water rafting trip, down the famous river Ganges, and all for under £5. Quite ridiculous. We drove along the cliff tops, from which the views were spectacular, just vast green forest all around, and the winding river Ganges far below, even the drive to the river bank was worth the £5, it was beautiful. After about 25 minutes of driving we arrived at our departure point.

After climbing out of the land rover, we walked down this windy little path until we were level with the Ganges, the water was racing at some pace, it looked pretty rough to me, although I didn't point that out to my Grandma at the time. We didn't have anything on us other than my phone, which was to grab a few pictures on. The guide for the white water rafting came over, and got us geared up with life jackets, helmets and paddles. I grabbed some photos of the surroundings as it really was beautiful and then a couple of pictures of me and my Grandma before we set of. The guide gave a quick, very brief explanation on how to paddle the boat and what to do if we fell out. Then no more than 30 seconds later, 8 of us were sat in the raft, pushing of from the bank, and afloat down the river.

The rafting was amazing, and my Grandma looked like she was loving it too, it wasn't just the rafting that was awesome, but the scenery really made for an incredible experience to. Just the thought of where we were, and who we were with, really made it incredible. We went up and down and over a few rapids, and then we came to a long smooth slow section, and the guide said we could jump in the water and float down. I was in within seconds, as it was hot, and looked refreshing, my Grandma was determined she wasn't getting out of the boat, although later on that day she was slinging herself of cliffs into the water… but more on that later. She sat there for a little while and then I put my head up and just saw her climbing over the edge of the boat, I remember thinking to myself, I knew she would get in. We both just laid on our backs with our toes and face to sky, floating down the river. It felt so peaceful, just floating down the Ganges, blue skies as you looked up, and the green mountains all around slightly seen in my peripheral vision. After about 15 minutes of floating peacefully down the river, the guide ordered us back into the boat. He pulled us all in one by one, we got back into position, and ready to take on the next set of rapids.

He would order the right side of the boat to paddle, then the left side, and sometimes everyone. My Grandma got it lucky, she got to sit in the middle and enjoy the ride. We went through the next two sets of rapids and then came to a slower section of water where we had to pull up to the bank, there were loads of rafts pulled up here, and he said it was for the cliff jumping. If we wanted to there were to high rock perches towering above the water, one was about 20ft and the other about 30ft. There were people stood at the top in small lines waiting to jump. We pulled the boat in and climbed over the edge onto the rocks. I presumed my Grandma wasn't going to be jumping because of her glasses and being unable to see, so I asked if she could hold my stuff while I went up and jumped of. I passed her over my phone and asked her to grab a video of me, and then made my way up to the 30ft jump with a few other people out of our boat. The thing was, there was no thinking about it, because there was a line of people waiting to jump behind you, once you were up there, it was almost impossible to turn around and go back, there literally was only one way down.

It was nearly my turn, there was just one guy in front of me, after a couple of minutes he finally found the courage and jumped, now it was my turn. It's the same as with any jump, it doesn't look to high when you're looking at it from below, but when you get to the top and look down and you have that 'oh shit feeling', regardless I jumped forward and landed into the freezing water. The current underneath was pretty strong and you had to be a pretty strong swimmer to be able to swim back to the bank. One of the guides was in a kayak in the water, he was constantly going and fetching people who couldn't make it and would end up floating down the river.

I managed to get pretty much all the way back to the bank, as to where I could stand up. I then stood up and took a glance up to the top of the rocks from where everyone was jumping. It's ridiculously coincidental that I looked up at that exact moment, but to my absolute shock my Grandma was mid air above the water, holding her nose and with her eyes closed.

I literally couldn't believe my eyes.

I remember standing in the water thinking, did my 68 year old Grandma just jump of a rock 20ft in the air into the river Ganges.

I guess I shouldn't have been so surprised, she hadn't really said no to anything the whole trip so far and always jumped at the opportunity to do anything. I didn't even have time to think about who had my phone. I was just about to swim out and help her in as the current was pretty strong, but one of the guides was already in the water and swam out to her. I'll let her tell you about how it happened. When she got to the bank and we were both on dry land, I said to her, 'what the hell Grandma, how did that happen' she said so calmly, 'oh I don't know, you only live once'. I was like oh fair enough. I was pretty impressed to be honest, she went and collected our phones of the kind girl that had been looking after them, and we clambered back into the raft ready for the final section of the river.

We tumbled up and over the rapids for another 20 minutes and went under the bridge that's situated in the middle of the city of Rishikesh. The water was a bit calmer here and we just floated down, almost peacefully. We then paddled into a little cove area in the bank, we all climbed out of the boat and helped pull it in. We handed in our helmets and life jackets, and the guides pointed us in the direction of the land rover. We walked up the steps on the bank of the river and all got a seat. It was pretty uncomfortable, about 8 people tightly squeezed into a land rover, wet and sweaty, it wasn't long until we were back at the tour excursion office, so wasn't that bad. We hopped out, grabbed our towels and dried ourselves off a little, we then decided to head back to the hostel to get a shower and quickly change our clothes before heading out and getting some lunch, as we were both starving.

We both decided on the little Buddha again, it was a little walk away, but we both thought worth it when we got there. It's only about a 10-15 minute walk, so it wasn't really that far anyway, and we knew the food would be good. I had already decided I was going to have momo again, the dumpling style dish with the soup, and my Grandma just had a sandwich. She was feeling a little bit ill. We weren't really sure why, and she didn't eat a lot of her sandwich, maybe just a few bites and then decided she had had enough. We think it was something to do with the heat, as we had been sat on the raft all morning without a hat on in the baking heat of India, being in and out of the water doesn't allow you to notice how hot it is either.

I also found out that my Grandma didn't have time to put sun cream on while we were rushing to get ready for the rafting, so she most definitely had sun stroke or that was what we both put it down to. She really wasn't feeling great at all. We sat there for another 20 minutes and had a drink and then we decided to head back as my Grandma wanted to go and lay down for a little while.

We began the walk back across the bridge, then up the hill towards the hostel. Grandma said she needed to stop a second as she really wasn't feeling great, then before I knew it, she was being sick over the side of the brick wall that we were stood up, it wasn't for long just maybe a minute or so, it was definitely being in the sun all day without a hat or sun cream. If I had done that when I was a kid I'm sure I would've got 'it's your own fault', but I was nicer. We still had to walk back to the hostel as there were no tuk tuks otherwise we would have to walk into Rishikesh town and that would've taken even longer. We thought it was sensible to get back and out of the sun, then my Grandma could rest for an hour or so. We also grabbed some water on the way so she could wash that sicky taste out of her mouth.

We got to the hostel about 5 minutes later, and Grandma decided she was going to go rest for a few hours. So of she went, I decided I would chill for a little bit, so I went to the rooftop, ordered a coffee and just sat and read for an hour or so. An hour later and still no sign of my Grandma, so I decided to go on a little walk. The route we took on our way rafting up the mountains looked beautiful, but we didn't really get the chance to look, or to take any pictures as we were crammed inside the land rover. So I decided to have a wander up and take some pictures, and take in the beautiful views. I left the hostel and walked up the road the same way that the land rover took us to the rafting spot, after about 20 minutes I arrived at a big clearing, basically a sandy lay-by which overlooked the Ganges and the mountains. The views were phenomenal vast green mountains either side of the river Ganges which you could see was racing from what must have been easily 500ft below. I sat on this big bit of sandy coloured stone and just took in the views for about 10 minutes until I felt a tap on my shoulder.

I turned around and there was this Indian man looking at me, he politely said hello, and then handed me an orange flavoured ice pole. It was basically the Indian version of a calippo. I presumed he got it from the small little ice cream stall that was situated in the corner of the lay-by and was manned by a young boy who mustn't have been more than 12 years old. It had old wooden wheels, and a steel frame. There was a big cool box sat inside the metal frame, and a make shift shade going over the top, I guess to cover the box from the sun. It got me thinking how crazily different our world is to theirs, it was a weekday and this young kid no older than 12 was selling ice creams on the side of the road, and had no doubt pushed it up this mammoth of a hill from the town, it really puts things into perspective.

I kindly said thank you for the ice pole, and we

spoke a little bit, he understood basic English so we could hold a reasonable conversation. Like where are you from, what do you do etc. After chatting for about 5 minutes he asked if he could have a photo with me. In my head I was thinking hell yeah, well worth the ice pole. He took about 10 different photos with me, maybe a little exaggeration, but it was a lot and then went back to his friends. I sat there again, eating my ice pole and taking in the beautiful views.

After another 10 minutes I decided I should probably head back to see how my Grandma was getting on, so I wandered back down the dusty road towards the hostel, it was much quicker getting back down, I was back at the hostel in 15 minutes.

I went to my room to put my mobile on charge and grab my book and headed to my Grandmas room. She was staying in a female only dorm, so I knocked on the door, and one of the other girls answered who we had gone for dinner with the night before, so they knew it was me looking for my Grandma. She was sat on the bed looking much better and just chatting to the two girls. I thought, oh that's great and then I headed up to the rooftop. About 20 minutes later Grandma came up and she said she was feeling much better, she just needed some time in the shade and to rest a little bit.

We then headed to the tourist office again to book our bus back to Delhi for the following day, we had decided to get an overnight bus despite our horrific experience of the previous one back to Delhi. And let me tell you, we triple checked to make sure there were no holy festivals, pilgrimages or events taking place along the route of our journey. We went back to the same tourism office and booked our tickets for the following evening at 9pm.

We weren't that hungry this evening I guess because we ate at about 3pm, so we just sat up on the rooftop all evening, spoke to people that came and went, played some cards, and just in general chilled out. We decided to have a lie in the next morning, or more I did. Just because I didn't know how much sleep we'd be getting on the overnight bus.

We were still up pretty late, and headed of to bed about 11pm. The later it got the more people came up to the rooftop, so there were plenty of people to talk to.

While I was in Rishikesh I had the opportunity to fulfil an ambition of my own. I had always fancied white-water rafting, but had never had the chance to do it.

Jake was a bit surprised at this, me being sixty-eight, but he was more than happy to go with me.

We had booked an afternoon trip, but when the day arrives plans changed. I was still sound asleep when Jake knocked on my dorm door. "Grandma, the weather is going to be bad this afternoon so we need to go this morning. We need to be there in half an hour". I jumped out of bed, threw on my clothes, grabbed a quick banana and off we went. I didn't even have time to put on sunscreen.

We made our way over to the agent office where a Land Rover waited to take us to our departure point on the riverbank. I had become a little concerned about loosing my glasses but was determined to find a solution so I did not miss out on the trip. The problem was solved by some cord-like elastic being tied around each of the side-arms and fastened at the back of my head. We had taken towels and a change of clothes, but we were told to leave them at the agency. I also left my Tilly hat, as I would be wearing a helmet in the boat. Phones, cameras and purses or wallets were the only exceptions, these being put into a sealed waterproof bag of the boat man during the ride. After a beautiful, scenic drive we arrived on the banks of the Ganges where two large inflatables awaited us.

We were kitted up with life jackets and helmets and had time for a photograph session before we were handed an oar each and told to make our way to the boats. There was space for eight people to paddle each boat, four per side, and as there were ten of us in our boat, I was ushered to sit in the middle along with one other person. Then we were off!

What an exhilarating ride! One minute the current would be carrying us along, the next our boatman would shout "Paddle, paddle paddle! Harder, Harder!" Once through a couple of rapids we came to a long stretch and most of the riders dropped into the water to float peacefully along. I stayed in the boat as I was unsure of being able to get back over the large tubes that formed the sides of the inflatable. However, after I saw one of the boatmen heave another passenger in I thought 'They can't leave me in the water through the next rapids, they HAVE to get me back in!' So, in I went, much to Jakes surprise. I had been adamant that I was not leaving the safety of the boat.

After another exciting ride through the rapids we arrived at a midway stop. There were stalls selling food and drink, hence being allowed to take our purses and wallets, but much more exciting for many, there were two cliffs. One was about thirty feet high, the other maybe twenty five, both crowded with people leaping into the Ganges. Once again, I was adamant that I was not going to jump, so I was left in charge of Jakes shoes and mobile phone. He asked me to take a video of him jumping with his mobile, but a combination of non-expertise and not being able to see properly because of the bright sunlight meant I think I got him on top of the cliff but I totally failed to follow him down!

After a while one of the young Indian girls from our boat asked me why I wasn't jumping. I showed her Jakes belongings and explained that I was looking after them while he jumped. "My friend doesn't want to jump any more. She will look after them". "I will guide you up, jump first, wait for you and guide you out". I was left with no more excuses. I handed over Jakes belongings and my shoes and glasses and off we went up to the cliff over the stony ground. The taller one was so crowded we would have never got to the front to jump so we decided on the slightly lower one. True to her words my guide jumped first. I went to the edge, looked down and thought 'my, that's very high! Can I really do this?' However, not only was my guide waiting expectantly in the water for me but I would never have been able to find my way down again without her.

I took a deep breath held my nose and jumped.

Wow.

I hit the water, my life jacket came up under my chin, I sank through the water and kicked for the surface. I was so exhilarated when I broke into the air I gave a whoop of triumph. Jake was flabbergasted. After my guide had seen me safely back to shore he came over.

'Grandma what are you like, one minute I saw you on the cliff, the next you're in the water. I didn't even see you jump, you amaze me!' Deep down I think he was quite proud of his old Grandma. I loved it so much I would have gone again, but it was time to leave. I offered to take a paddle for the last leg of the journey but was told, 'no, you are the grandmother you sit here', so I finished the journey as I had started it, in style. Strangely enough it was done in a way that I didn't feel old and decrepit, just respected.

On landing we were taken back to the agency to collect our belongings. The towel and change of clothes had been a waste of time as we were almost dry, so we just made out way back to the hostel.

After changing into fresh clothes we decided to go to the little Buddha for some lunch. I should have felt very hungry after all that activity on a virtually empty stomach, but in fact I was starting to feel rather queasy. I thought maybe it was due to a touch of the sun, having had neither sun cream or a hat all morning. On the river the sun was very intense. By the time I got the restaurant I was feeling really rough! I

*ordered a light meal and a cool lemon-mint
drink, hoping it would make me feel better.
However, I could only manage three or four
mouthfuls, so Jake again stepped in and
finished it for me. We set of back to the hostel,
but I got worse and worse as the journey
progressed. I really felt like I wouldn't be able
to make it back.*

*However we were way of the beaten track, so
hailing a passing tuk tuk was not an option.
About half way home I felt I could go no further.
I needed to sit down for a while, so we sat on
the end of a wall on the other side of which was
a steep hillside. After a few minutes my stomach
finally rebelled, and I turned around and
vomited all down the hillside. Unlike in
England, the passers by took absolutely no
notice. To Indian people, those things happen,
especially to Europeans. However I now felt
100% better and was able to walk back to the
hostel comfortably. I still don't know what made
me feel the way I did, but one thing was for
certain, Rishikesh is dry, so it certainly wasn't
alcohol.*

*When we got back Jake wanted to walk back
along the path at the route we had driven to the*

river. There had been some spectacular views on the way and he wanted another look. I would have loved to too, but decided and hour in bed would be more beneficial. I woke up several hours later feeling back to normal and ready for the evenings excursion. Thankfully I had no repetition of the afternoons unfortunate events.

Chapter 15 – Day 4 Rishikesh

This was our final day in Rishikesh, the day we were due to go and get the bus back to Delhi. I felt kind of sad about leaving Rishikesh, I wasn't too keen on Delhi. It was interesting, and had some amazing parts to it and beautiful temples to see, but Rishikesh had a sort of charm about it.

We woke up at a reasonable time, and packed our bags as we had to be checked out of the hostel room by 10am. We had decided that we would leave the hostel at about 7.30pm as it would take 30 minutes to get into the town centre, which is where the bus station was, and then it would give us an hour spare just in case.

After checking out and handing in the keys to our rooms we went up to the rooftop to grab some breakfast, a few of the guys from the night before were up there and asked if we wanted to walk up to this waterfall with them. It was about an hours hike in total, up steep steps. It was roasting hot so made it seem a lot worse. My Grandma had decided not to come, as she thought it wouldn't be enjoyable for herself, and after getting sunstroke the day before, she was quite happy relaxing and reading her book. I double checked with her, and she really didn't seem to mind, so she stayed at the hostel, read her book and did some crosswords. While myself and a couple of people from the hostel decided to hike up to this waterfall.

We headed out of the hostel and walked up the road for about 25 minutes, the same way I had gone previously to look at the views, but after about 10 minutes we turned of up this dirt road and walked up there for another 15-20 minutes. It was hot, I think the temperature was around 38c. I was dripping with sweat, there were a few other people walking, all sweating just as much as we were. There was the option at the bottom of the dirt track to get in a car up to the main starting point for the waterfall trail, but we decided not to pay and walk.

After about 30 minutes walking from starting at the hostel we got to the beginning of the trail. The trail was busy, it looked like a lot of people drove up to here, parked their cars and then just walked up to the waterfall from the actual beginning. We began walking up to the waterfall, it was a thin dirt path, probably thick enough to fit two people side by side, there were steps built in at certain points along the way to help, as the path was pretty slippy from all the rain.

We continued walking for about another 30 minutes until we got to the top, stopping a couple of times on the way to catch our breath, and grab some water. When we got to the top there was a big pool of what looked like ice cold water, and the waterfall behind pouring over the top into the pool below. The water look so refreshing, especially as the outside air was so hot, it wasn't long before we had all dropped our bags and jumped in the water, it was so refreshing, we must have stayed in there for a good 20 minutes.

After chilling out in the water for a good 20 minutes we jumped out, none of us brought towels, so we just had to let the air dry us off. We sat down just above the waterfall for a little while, allowing time for our feet to dry so we could put our socks and trainers on. It was really scenic around the waterfall, other than for the many people sat around and in the water pool at the bottom of the waterfall, it did kind of ruin the picturesqueness of the place. Lush green forest all around, and situated in the middle of it this ice cold 15 foot high waterfall. It really would have been a peaceful place if it was quite, but it made for quite a tourist destination, they even charged us to get up to it. There was a little man sat in a box at the entrance to the waterfall trail and you had to pay him, only foreigners did though, locals didn't have to pay. It wasn't a lot, 50p or something like that.

After letting ourselves dry a little and putting our shoes and socks on, we decided to start wandering back down the trail to the hostel. It was much easier and faster going down, although the humidity still caused us to sweat ridiculous amounts. It wasn't even worth putting a t-shirt back on, as within a few minutes it would be damp with sweat again. Within about 15 minutes we were at the bottom of the trail at the dirt road, and within another 20 we were back at the hostel.

I went upstairs to see how my Grandma was doing and she seemed quite content just chilling out reading her book. She asked me how the hike up to the waterfall was, and we just sat and chilled for a little bit before deciding to go and get some lunch.

I decided to have another shower, seeing as I had just hiked to this waterfall and was covered in sweat yet again, and then we headed out.

It was about 3pm by now, so it was our last meal in Rishikesh, and I'm sure you can already guess where we went… the little Buddha. I'm pretty sure that was probably one of the only restaurants we ate at while we were in Rishikesh, other than the hostel. But it was good food, and had amazing views overlooking the Ganges, so why change it. We wandered down the same little road to the start of the bridge, wandered over the bridge with all the other people, scooters and cows that were crossing, and then back up the muddy road the other side until we came to the steel stairs that went up to the little Buddha.

I went and got Palak Paneer again with a garlic naan and my Grandma got the same. It was probably one of the best dishes I had throughout my time in India, and I think my Grandma would agree, although she seemed to enjoy all the food. We also got a juice, I got a minty, green tea lemon flavoured drink and I think my Grandma got a mango style one, they were both delicious. We sat in the two chairs that were right up against the bamboo fence at the end of the cafe, both overlooking right out over the Ganges, it really was beautiful. Our food came and we soon scoffed it down, dipping the naan into the smooth slightly spicy, spinach flavoured curry… which I know sounds disgusting, but it really was amazing and I'd definitely recommend it. After eating our food and taking in the view for a final few minutes we decided it was time to walk back to the hostel.

We had been sat in the little Buddha for over 2 hours just talking, taking in the views and reminiscing on what an adventure we'd had in Rishikesh. We kind of looked back at it with gob smacked faces.

It was one of those did that really happen kind of memories.

For me it was like, did I really do all that with my 68 year old Grandma.

And for her it was like, did I really do that with my 20 year old Grandson.

It was a crazy thought.

We left the little Buddha, stopped at the local shop, I guess similar to a convenience store. We picked up water, a couple mango juices and then some snacks for the bus ride back and for the rest of the evening, as I knew I would get hungry later, that was a given.

We got back to the hostel for about 6, giving us about an hour before we had to leave. We both decided to get showers again, get dressed into the clothes we were travelling in and then chill until 19.30 and it was time to leave.

19.30 came and it was time to grit our teeth and tackle another night bus. We were both hoping it was nothing like the last one. I'm sure it wasn't going to be as we had been reassured numerous times that there were definitely no festivals going on along our route. And as my Grandma kept saying 'nothing can be worse than last time, it can only be better'. Which was true.

We found out that a couple of girls from Texas were travelling on the same bus as us, we had met them a few days ago. They had been staying in the same room as my Grandma, and they came for dinner with us a few times to the little Buddha.

We decided to travel all as a group to the bus stop, so we got a taxi and headed into Rishikesh bus station, there was a little traffic on the way down the mountain to the actual town of Rishikesh, but there always was, that's why we had planned to leave a good hour early. It took us about 45 minutes to get to Rishikesh bus station.

We were there about 45 minutes early so we decided to grab a seat in one of these little cafes, and me and my Grandma grabbed a cola, we sat there for about 30 minutes, just talking and watching the hectic world go by. It was about 20:45, and we decided we should go and look for our bus, we walked into the bus station and saw a bus with Delhi on it, so we went and sat down next to it and waited for the driver. It got to about 20:55 and there was still no sign of a bus driver or anyone waiting for the bus and I began to get a little nervous.

The thing with this bus station was, there was no office, or place where you could go and speak to anyone, you just had to kind of guess, or shout 'Delhi'. Then someone would wave you over, you'd show them your ticket, and they would say yes or no depending on whether or not that was your bus.

I gave it another minute and nothing changed, and I thought I needed to go look around otherwise we were going to miss this bus. I got up and said to Grandma I was going to look around. I left my backpack with the others, jumped up and started like a gentle jog around this bus station.

After going around the bus station and finding nothing, I headed to the main road and noticed there was another section to the station, a much smaller area but there were a few buses with there lights on. There also seemed to be a few more people. I ran over to all the buses that had people queuing to get on and shouted 'Delhi', I tried one and he said no, then another and I got a yes.

I showed him our wrinkled up paper tickets and he said yes.

What a relief.

Thank god for that I thought, good job I checked otherwise we would've been spending another night in Rishikesh.

I said to him, '2 minutes, my friends' and pointed in the direction of where the others were sitting, he nodded and said 'yes, no problem'. I ran back to grab the others. They jumped up, I helped Grandma with her backpack, and we all quickly paced around the corner to where the bus was parked.

I thought we were sat there for 30 minutes doing nothing and we're still bloody rushing for this bus. We got to the bus, and he said 'Delhi' we gave him our backpacks which he slung under the bus, climbed up the rusty steel steps and found our seats. Funnily enough the bus still didn't leave for another 15 minutes.

15 minutes went by and then the old bus engine started up again, and slowly rolled out of the station onto the road. I pulled out my book and read for about an hour until it was 10pm, and then put in my ear plugs and tried to get some sleep. My Grandma stayed up reading until about 11pm I think.

The next day Jake wanted to visit a waterfall he'd heard about with some of the other travellers. It sounded wonderful, but I was told that after being dropped off visitors faced a steep scramble. Unsure of how I would cope with this I decided to spend a quite day at the hotels with my book and my puzzles. Also I didn't want to push my luck after the previous afternoon. Jake had a marvellous time, but said that I had made a wise decision. All I could do was listen enviously to this stories of the fun they had in what sounded like a beautiful place. That evening we all went down to the little Buddha for a last meal before we all went our separate ways, and Jake and I had to head back to Delhi for our last two days.

We had learned our lesson in Agra, so this time we travelled on an official government bus. What a difference. We travelled overnight again, and although the bus wasn't a sleeper it was air-conditioned. In fact the reclining seats were much more comfortable than the bunks in the previous bus. We had a very smooth ride and I slept just as much, if not more than I have ever done before while travelling. Furthermore, we actually arrived on time and made our way back to Joey's hostel in time for breakfast.

Chapter 16 – Day 5 New Delhi

I had a pretty restless nights sleep, I think I woke up around 7 or 8 times throughout the whole journey. I'm not sure why I just couldn't get into a deep enough sleep to nod off for a few hours, I was up every hour or so.

Grandma said she slept well, she said that she didn't really wake up through the night. The bus arrived into Delhi actually before schedule, we arrived at Delhi bus station at about 5.15am. I tried to wake myself up and get my head switched on for the Delhi rush, but I was super tired. Having been in and out of sleep all night, and sat not on the most comfortable bus, I was pretty knackered. I can hardly complain though, we arrived early and it was a million times better than our other experience of an Indian night bus. We were just happy to have arrived early.

We got off the bus and grabbed our backpacks from underneath. The two girls we met in Rishikesh were staying in a different hostel in Delhi to us. We said goodbye and wished them the best on the rest of their travels. We then proceeded to find ourselves a tuk tuk to the hostel, there were loads of them waiting for everyone to get of the buses, so we were hardly short on choice. We haggled with a few drivers until we got a fair price. We knew exactly what was fair, as we had been in Delhi for 4 days before, so there was none of that having no idea what a fair price is when you first arrive into a country, and you're just guessing, hoping you're not being ripped off.

After haggling with a few drivers for a few minutes, one agreed to take us for the price we wanted. We hopped in and off we went back to Joey's hostel. It took us about 15 minutes and we pulled up outside where our journey had first begun.

It was weird being back here, at the first hostel we stayed in, the place we started our Indian adventure.

It felt crazy to think that we were going home tomorrow.

We got out of the tuk tuk and wandered up the dusty sand road which went up to the side of the main road, it was still pretty cool outside, and there weren't many people about. This street in the day was ridiculously busy. Filled with people, scooters buzzing around, animals and children. We got to the entrance to the hostel, walked up the stairs and went into the reception area.

It looked like the guys that worked at reception were just getting up, they opened up for us and took our names and booking confirmations, they said our rooms wouldn't be ready for another hour or so. So we both sat down on the sofas in the hostel. I laid out on one of the sofas and fell asleep for around an hour and a half, waking up at about 7.30am, and I think my Grandma just read her book, she wasn't that tired as she got a pretty good sleep on the bus.

As soon as I hit the sofa my eyes started to close, so I just went with it, laid my head on a pillow and got some rest. When I woke at about 7.30am, breakfast was just starting. We decided to make the most of our final day in Delhi, so we decided to get some breakfast, get showers and get on with the day.

Breakfast for me consisted of coco pops, tea and some bread with jam. My room still wasn't ready but my Grandmas was so we put both of our bags in there. I grabbed my towel and some clean clothes, and headed to the showers. Showered, put on clean clothes, sun creamed up and was ready to go. I grabbed another tea and checked my phone while I waited for my Grandma, it was only 5 minutes more and she was ready to go to.

We left the hostel at about 8.30am and it was still quiet outside. The streets seemed to be really quiet throughout the day and then start getting busier in the afternoon/evenings around 5/6pm. Me and Grandma put this down to it being too hot to be out in the day, it was much cooler once the sun had gone down, that's when it seemed to get busier and the streets would liven up. People would set up their stalls, selling food, talking and socialising, buying their shopping, and playing cards on the side of the street.

We decided today that we would go and do some shopping, head to the markets and see what deals we could find. My Grandma wanted to get gifts for everyone back at home, and I wanted to just have a look around and see what I could find.

We jumped in a tuk tuk and headed to this market called Chandni Chownk. I had done a little research before, and this market was supposed to be good. Lots of choice for men and women's clothing, jewellery, ornaments, spices, furniture, literally everything we could want, and it wasn't to far away from where our hostel was situated so we thought it was perfect.

We arrived, climbed out of the tuk tuk and then wandered to the market. The market was basically in a long straight row, and it was a mixture of shops and stalls. It started out as shops, there were probably about 20 in a line. Then there was a little market section in the middle with stalls that were put up with a steel frames and wooden planks. The planks then covered with some sort of colourful blanket and the goods of whatever they were selling on the top. Then the final section was another row of about 25-30 stores. On the other side of the road their were restaurants, bars and even a McDonald's, which we retreated to if we needed a blast of air con.

We started at one end and wandered all the way down, going in every store that took our fancy and haggling down the price if there was anything we liked the look of. A lot of the stalls were selling very similar items so we kind of had the advantage, as if it wasn't a price that we found reasonable, we would just walk for 30 seconds and try the next shop and so on. After about 2-3 hours of shopping and wandering round the markets, we both had our hands full of bags. My Grandma had successfully bought a gift for everyone, and I had bought a few things that took my fancy, from an Indian looking cushion to a pair of black harem pants.

By now it was starting to get hot outside, it was about midday by the time we had finished with our shopping, and we noticed a little bar across the road, we both gave each other that kind of 'hell yeah' look again, and wandered over towards the bar. We got up to the door of the bar and pushed it open and much to our surprise the place was air-conditioned to the max. The only other place that was air-conditioned was McDonald's. We used to go and sit in McDonald's when we needed a break from the sun, we would just grab a cold drink each and sit in there when it got that unbearable outside.

After entering the bar we knew it was going to be pretty expensive, anywhere that was air conditioned in India was going to be expensive, it was almost as if you were paying for the privilege of it. The waiter came over and handed us two menus, we decided to get a jug of beer as we knew we would drink more than one each and it worked out cheaper to get a jug than four.

The beer came, and it was pretty good. It was cold and it was beer, so it couldn't really be bad. It wasn't actually that expensive, it was for India, but not comparative to Europe, the jug came to about £8. Which wasn't really that bad at all, but when we were living of £12 a day including accommodation, transport and food, I'm sure you can see how we thought it was expensive.

It was really nice, just drinking cold beer, relaxing in the air-conditioned bar, and talking about our favourite parts of the Adventure.

It felt crazy that we were going home tomorrow morning, flying back to London.

In one way I was looking forward to getting back, getting back to the things we take for granted back home. Like food that didn't give me stomach ache, a nice shower, a comfortable bed, walking around and not profusely sweating. I was kind of looking forward to getting home. I felt India was one of those places, it was beautiful and such an incredible experience, but I felt like I needed a holiday from my holiday. We were on the go constantly, seeing new things, walking miles each day, and the heat really did make us super tired.

But then on the other hand I was going to miss it, miss the adventures and miss spending quality time with my Grandma and having these awesome experiences together every day.

We ordered another jug of beer and just enjoyed the comfort of the bar for another hour or so. We paid the waiter and headed back outside to the heat. As I opened the door the heat hit me right in the face, it was around 1pm now, so the heat had really picked up, it must have been around 40c, and it wasn't only the heat, but the humidity that really made it feel hot and sticky.

We jumped in a tuk tuk across the other side of the road and headed back to the hostel, we thought we would go and drop our shopping off at the hostel, maybe chill out for a little bit and then head to this temple that looked pretty cool for the afternoon.

We shot in-between the traffic and after about 15 minutes arrived back at the hostel. We dropped everything we bought at the market back into our rooms and just slumped out on the sofas for a little while, my Grandma reading her book, and I was just chilling on my phone.

After about an hour of chilling we decided to go and check out this temple which was about 25 minutes away from the hostel. We had pretty much done everything we wanted to do in Delhi, we did most of it the first time round, and we had already been to the markets and done some shopping, so there wasn't really much left for us to do.
We took a tuk tuk and arrived at this temple roughly around 25 minutes later. As usual it took us a while to explain where it was, even with showing the driver a map it still caused for a little confusion, but we got there in the end… around 35 minutes later.

The temple wasn't really that great, I thought it would have been bigger and it was pretty run down, almost like an empty church, but we had a look around anyway. We walked around the temple for around 10 minutes as there really wasn't much to see. We decided between ourselves that there was really no point in going back yet, we might as-well have a wander around the area and get a little lost. We knew the train station that the hostel was outside, so all we had to do to get back was jump in a tuk tuk and mention this station.

We left the entrance to the temple and wandered down the street, it was starting to get a little cooler now, and by a little cooler I mean around 30c and not the scorching 40c of the mid day heat. So the temperature was pretty perfect for just having a wander around the streets. We literally had no idea where we were. It seemed we had stumbled across a quite wealthy part of New Delhi as there were houses with huge gates and fences around them, and some quite flashy cars driving around. The area itself seemed a lot more modern and clean, there wasn't as much litter on the floor and on either side of the road there was a big, pink brick pavement. Whereas in other areas of Delhi it was hard to distinguish a pavement even at all.

The houses that were fenced seemed to be 2-3

stories high so were pretty huge. They all seemed to be in a similar square shape, and surrounded by a similar size wall leaving them with a small garden around the outside of the house.

We continued walking for another hour around the suburbs of what it seemed to be a wealthy part of New Delhi until we came across what felt a lot like a shopping high street. There were shops on either side of the road, almost western looking shops. And it was really busy, not that anywhere in Delhi wasn't I guess. There were also a few little carts selling various items such as juices and food.

It was now about 4.30pm after our brief exploration of the temple and our wander around Delhi, so we decided we would head back and chill out before our early flight tomorrow. I noticed a momo stall a little further ahead, and they were super cheap, I think 12 for £1 or something like that. I decided to get some for my dinner. Grandma decided she was going to order something once we got back to the hostel a little later. There were microwaves at the hostel so I could heat them up.

I was sure to ask for the vegetarian ones, as I had tried to stay away from meat while I was in Delhi, just for my stomachs sake. He grabbed a big metal spoon with holes in it, and scooped me 12 out of the hot water, he let them drain for a little before putting them into a paper bag. He then gave me three different sauce, a green one, a red one and a white one. They were all a variant of some sort of chilli sauce, the green and red were my favourite, this was the first time I had been given the white one, and I didn't like it at all. It was like a creamy floury chilli sauce, and it wasn't to my liking. The other two were amazing, both chilli sauces, the green one a little sweeter than the red. He put the lids on the sauces and put it all into a tightly sealed plastic bag and then put this in a carrier bag. I gave him my £1 worth of Indian rupee which was about 100 rupees at the time, and we headed down the street to find a tuk tuk back.

We got back to the hostel about 30 minutes later, who knows where we had wandered to, but it was definitely in the wrong direction. Not that it mattered, it's not like it cost us any more in the tuk tuk, or we had to walk back.

We decided that evening we would just chill

out, grab some beers, play some cards and get an early night before our flight the following day.

We chilled out in the hostel for a few minutes, put my momo in the fridge, then we headed out to grab a couple of beers each. This would be the last time we headed down this street in the evening, tomorrow morning it would be dead as if no-one even lived here. We wandered down the dirt path, dodging dogs, scooters, people and the occasional donkey, until we got to the beer store. We grabbed a couple of beers each and made the same walk back.

My Grandma decided she was going to order some food as she didn't fancy momo. She grabbed one of the menus and decided she was going to have palak paneer our favourite dish. She went to the receptionist who ordered it for her, she then gave him the cash and he would collet it for her when it came. We also decided against ordering a taxi to the airport the next day. We thought we would risk it and just get a tuk tuk, there was bound to be one that would get us to the airport. Our flight was at 8.30am, so we had to be up at 5am to get to the airport for about 6.

Grandmas food came, and I heated up my momo, we pretty much shared the dinner. Going just about halves each on both. We stayed up till about 9pm, playing cards and drinking our beers on one of the wooden tables in the hostel. The living area of the hostel was pretty small, and once everyone was in there, there wasn't a great deal of room.

We then packed up the cards, cleared away our beers and headed to our rooms. We both decided to pack that evening just leaving out everything we needed for the morning.

We set an agreed time to meet downstairs.

5.30am ready to leave.

Then went to our separate dorms for our final night in India.

Our last two days in Delhi were mainly spent shopping. We had seen no point in carrying gifts and souvenirs all over India. We found a little market with many different stalls where the vendors were willing to barter. I bought a small leather rucksack to replace my shoulder bag at £3 and earrings at 50p a pair. We also returned to a wide shopping street I had seen on our previous visit to Delhi. It was here we made perhaps what was our greatest find, a cool, air conditioned McDonald's, where we could drink delicious iced coffee and examine our purchases. It was in here that I switched from my useless shoulder bag to my new rucksack. The shops along here all had signs that read 'no bargaining'.

We went into one shop selling clothing looking for the baggy harem style pants that we called elephant pants, simply because they had an elephant pattern on them. We felt his prices were a bit to high so we told him, 'no we are not paying that as down the road they are only 200 rupees each', about £2.

After some discussion he agreed to sell them to us at the same price. I think it helped that we wanted about 10 pairs between us. I also brought some small patchwork animals for my other three grandchildren at stocking fillers.

Along a narrow alley we found stalls selling spices and street food. This is where Jake brought his spices at about a quarter of the *price that I paid in Jaipur. At one stall we stood and watched the stall holder deep frying larger spicy samosas. We decided that they would make the perfect lunch, so as soon as they were ready we brought some. At 10p each it seemed rude to only buy one, so brought two, but as usual it was too much for me so Jake had to eat one! Another life saving find was an air conditioned bar where we shared a pitcher of beer between us.*

After shopping we went for a wander around and found a small park with two ancient temple like buildings in it. It was here I nearly came to a sticky end. Following the usual road safety regime of waiting for a small gap in the traffic and dashing across Jake suddenly said 'come on Grandma'. Lacking concentration, I was a bit slow of the mark and therefore had to rush a little faster than usual.

Chapter 17 – Coming Home

We were both up bright and early and were ready to leave by about 5.20am. I paid for the hostel as we forgot to pay the night before, and thought there was no harm in leaving early so we headed down the deep brick staircase that led up to the hostel and left our first and final hostel in India.

It was a beautiful morning, there was a cool breeze and the sun was just beginning to rise. It was quite refreshing to step outside and it not be boiling hot. We wandered down the dirt track along the side of the busy main road until we got to where there were usually loads of tuk tuk's parked.

There weren't any there at the moment, but we didn't think (hoped) it would be long until one passed us.

About 5 minutes went by and one come racing down the almost quiet road, we waved over at it and he yanked his steering wheel to the right and darted across the road at us. We said to him 'the airport', put our bags on the seats and got in. It took us about 30 minutes to get to the airport and it was quite a nice ride.

The road were reasonably quiet, the sun was rising, and it was nice and cool, so my back wasn't sticking to the leather seats of the tuk tuk. The scenery was also beautiful, we crossed this long bridge that went over a wide river. The banks were a muddy green, there were cows grazing and people walking up and down the long green banks. It was the type of scenery where, everywhere you looked something new would be happening. The type of scenery you could watch for hours and always find something new and interesting to look at. It was made even more beautiful by the sun rising just over the banks of the river, giving it this almost movie like shine.

We pulled into the departures area of New Delhi airport, we put our backpacks on our backs, paid the tuk tuk driver and headed to check in.

We were flying with Turkish airlines, who were great. We decided to check in on these do it yourself computers as the check in queue was pretty long, then we could just head to bag drop and drop our bags. Making the whole process a lot easier. After putting in a few details such as booking reference and flight number and then scanning our passports a boarding pass was printed out the bottom. We both double checked to make sure our boarding passes were correct and then queued up in the bag drop line.

The bag drop line was relatively small compared to the check in one, and it moved down a lot quicker as all you needed to do was show your boarding pass and give them your bags. It took around 25 minutes for us to get our bags dropped off and then we headed through security.

After getting through security we had about an hour until our flight left, we decided to go and get a coffee as we were bound to get breakfast on the flight. The first flight was from New Delhi to Istanbul and then switching from there back to London.

We had a coffee and spoke about our travels, laughing at everything we had done and some of the stuff that had happened until it was time for us to head to the gate and board the plane.

The journey home was nice, it was nice to enjoy a couple of films and eat some nice food. I know it was only plane food but it was still nice to have some European food inside me. I had a couple of coffees and just chilled out, the first flight was about 6 hours, the second only 4.

We had a layover of around an hour in Istanbul, but it went really quick. By the time everyone was of the plane it was time to be getting back on it again. Luckily this time the plane arrived on schedule, so we weren't stressing that we were going to miss it like on our inbound plane.

Again on the second flight we watched a couple of films and had another meal. We arrived back into London in the afternoon. After collecting our bags and Grandma remembering what hers looked like after 3 weeks of using it, we headed through security, then outside to the train station. We had to get the train back to Peterborough which is about an hours drive home as everyone was working. The train journey took us about 2 hours in total, from leaving the airport on the tube to Kings Cross station and then getting the mainline train from there to Peterborough took another 45 minutes.

Dad was waiting for us as we stepped out of the train station. As we chucked our backpacks in the back of the car and climbed in it felt kind of surreal. Here we were back where we started. It hadn't seemed 5 minutes since we left, since we were getting our backpacks out of the car and walking into the airport. Now here we were heading home, after nearly 3 weeks backpacking around northern India with my Grandma, we were home.

What a crazy experience, it almost didn't feel real, it all happened so quickly.

Within the space of 5 weeks, I was going to India on my own, had invited my Grandma, she had said yes, we had got everything booked, spent 16 days in this crazy country, and we were back.

What an adventure.

One that I'm sure we'll both never forget.

Eventually the day came when we had to return home. It was an early morning flight so we were in bed in good time the evening before, to try and catch a few hours sleep. There was an England football match on TV the evening so I was getting up just as a newly arrived couple arrived couple were coming to bed after watching the match. We stopped at the desk to pay for our three nights accommodation. Unusually we had not been asked to pay on arrival. Events were to prove that this had been a mistake. The young lad was half asleep and things got somewhat confused, with Jake and I working out who owed what. Being only half awake myself we were halfway to the airport before I realised I was 500 rupees short in my change. Five pounds doesn't buy much in England but it was a lot in India and meant we were limited as to what we could buy at the airport. I handed over all my rupees to Jake and we shared what we had left. It was a salutary lesson, concentrate when paying bills, no matter how early in the morning!

Luckily breakfast was served on the plane, along with other meals. On the return flight we had three or four hours in Istanbul, plenty of time for coffee and airport shopping. Having no euros, my credit card came into its own, as the shop owners didn't want to take sterling. After enjoying a coffee in Nero's of all places, I treated myself to some Turkish goodies such as Turkish delights and dates.

We arrived back in England after an uneventful flight and started the last leg of our journey, the train ride home. Jake had booked his ticket when he booked the holiday, of course, so mine was bought over the internet from Rishikesh. Luckily he got the last seat on the train he was on. This meant we weren't even in the same carriage, never mind next to each other, on the train from Kings Cross the Peterborough. The seat next to me had not been reserved until after Peterborough, so we could have sat next to each other after all.

Jakes dad, Lee, was meeting us at Peterborough so we both sent him a text when we were getting near. As Lee had an hours drive to get to us Jake said ' I bet he'll be late'. In this he did his dad a great injustice. Lee was a welcome sight as we left the station weighed down with backpacks and front-packs.

With great relief we loaded all our baggage into the boot, sank into the comfort of the Cherokees leather seats and headed for home!

Printed in Great Britain
by Amazon